ENGLISCH
GRUNDKURS
Lehrerhandbuch

für technische Berufe

Ernst Klett Verlag
Stuttgart · Düsseldorf · Leipzig

ENGLISCH
GRUNDKURS für technische Berufe
Lehrerhandbuch

von Wolfram Büchel
     Rosemarie Mattes
     Hartmut Mattes
     Mary Schäfer
     Dr. Wolfgang Schäfer

Sprachzentrum - Centre de langues
Kinzigstr. 35 · D-77694 Kehl
Tel. 07851/73069
Tel. 00.49.7851/73060

1. Auflage   A 1 ⁵⁴³²¹ | 2005 2004 2003 2002

Alle Drucke dieser Auflage können im Unterricht nebeneinander benutzt werden. Die letzte Zahl bezeichnet das Jahr dieses Druckes.
© Ernst Klett Verlag GmbH, Stuttgart 2002. Alle Rechte vorbehalten.
Internetadresse: http://www.klett-verlag.de

Redaktion: Volker Wendland

Einbandgestaltung: Elmar Feuerbach

Druck: Schnitzer Druck GmbH, Korb. Printed in Germany.

ISBN 3-12-809410-1

Vorwort

Der Unterricht in technischem Englisch stellt an die Kolleginnen und Kollegen, die das Fach unterrichten, erhöhte Anforderungen. Nur die wenigsten haben i.d.R. zusätzlich zum Anglistikstudium ein Studium in einem technischen Fach absolviert. Zudem wird kaum jemand mit allen im Grundkurs behandelten Themen vertraut sein – sie reichen ja von der einfachen Bürokommunikation und der Computertechnik bis hin zu den Grundlagen im Maschinenbau und zur Elektrotechnik.

Um den Unterrichtenden die Arbeit mit dem Grundkurs zu erleichtern, werden daher im Lehrerhandbuch zusätzliche Informationen angeboten, die in einfacher Form in verschiedene Bereiche der Technik – wie z.B. in den Bereich der Werkzeugmaschinen – einführen.

Darüber hinaus gibt es eine Fülle von Hinweisen ⓘ für den Unterricht mit leistungsstärkeren bzw. leistungsschwächeren Klassen sowie Vorschläge für alternative Aufgaben.

Der Aufbau des Lehrerhandbuches orientiert sich am Schülerbuch. Nach einer kurzen Inhaltsübersicht zur jeweiligen Unit folgt der Lösungsschlüssel (ⓚ = key). Im Anhang gibt es einen fotokopierbaren Teil mit zusätzlichen Aufgaben zur Vertiefung des Stoffes. Zu den fotokopierbaren Aufgaben zählen Wortschatzübungen in Form von Kreuzworträtseln, Einsetzaufgaben und Abbildungen von Werkzeugmaschinen, von denen einige Teile zu beschriften sind. Das Lehrerhandbuch schließt mit Vorschlägen zu Klassenarbeiten und einer kleinen Übersicht, in der wesentliche Unterschiede zwischen amerikanischem und britischem Englisch veranschaulicht werden.

Inhaltsübersicht   Seite

Vorwort

Unit 1 The new job Starter	5
A Welcome to Leeds Airport!	6
B Arrival at Power Engines Ltd	6
C Introducing the company	7
D Grammar revision	8
Unit 2 Office work Starter	9
A Office routine	9
B Telephoning	11
C Letter writing	13
D Grammar revision	16
Unit 3 Information technologies – Electronic communication Starter	17
A Hardware	18
B Software	22
C The Internet - Communication and information	26
D Grammar revision	31

Unit 4 Mechanical engineering – Tools Starter — 32
A Shop floors and joining methods — 33
B Machine tools and power tools — 35
C Safety regulations in a workshop — 41
D Grammar revision — 42

Unit 5 Troubleshooting, maintenance and warranties Starter — 43
A Troubleshooting – A column drill — 44
B DIY Power Tools Manual — 45
C Maintenance and warranty — 45
D Grammar revision — 49

Unit 6 Electrical engineering Starter — 50
A Some basic facts about electricity — 51
B Electricity applied — 54
C New technologies: Hydrogen and the fuel cell — 55
D Grammar revision — 57

Unit 7 Properties of materials and quality standards (ISO) Starter — 58
A Describing products — 58
B Engineering materials — 60
C Measurement and quality control (ISO) — 63
D Grammar revision — 65

Unit 8 Energy and the environment Starter — 66
A Global warming and the greenhouse effect — 67
B Renewable sources of energy — 69
C Nuclear fission and nuclear fusion — 73
D Grammar revision — 74

Unit 9 Business trips Starter — 77
A A business trip — 77
B Arriving in Philadelphia — 82
C Cultural aspects — 83
D Grammar revision — 85

Unit 10 Finding a job in Europe Starter — 86
A Our workplace is changing — 87
B Working in Europe — 87
C Jobs, job application and interview — 90
D Grammar revision — 91

Files — 92

Fotokopierbare Materialien — 95

Fotokopierbare Materialien: Lösungen — 108

Some differences in vocabulary between British and American English — 112

Unit 1
The new job

Oliver, ein junger deutscher Arbeitnehmer, entschließt sich, ein Arbeitsverhältnis in Großbritannien anzutreten. Bei der Suche nach einem geeigneten Arbeitsplatz bedient er sich entsprechender Internetseiten. Nach erfolgreicher Bewerbung wird im *Teil A* die Ankunft am Flughafen Leeds beschrieben. *Teil B* schildert Olivers ersten Kontakt mit seinem künftigen Arbeitgeber bei der Firma Power Engines Ltd. Hierbei werden typische Redewendungen, die während des ersten Kontaktes im englischsprachigen Raum gebräuchlich sind, eingeübt. Im *Teil C* wird Oliver die Firma vorgestellt (Organigramm und Lageplan). Die Grammatik im *Teil D* dient zur Wiederholung wichtiger Zeiten (Present Tense, Present Perfect und Past Tense) anhand von situativen berufsbezogenen Übungen.

Starter

a
1. applicants
2. employment opportunities
3. desirable
4. per annum
5. contact
6. quote
7. file
8. varied
9. requirements
10. challenging
11. fringe benefits
12. thrive

b

1. Oliver decided to apply for the position as mechanical engineer, because he has a degree in mechanical engineering. Another reason might be the offer of a company car.
2. Individual answers by the students are expected.
3. You should write your curriculum vitae and send it to Power Engines via e-mail.
4. If they are interested in your application, they will invite you for a job interview. If not, the application will be registered and kept on file.

c   Schülerantworten

Bei einer leistungsstärkeren Klasse kann hier ein Gespräch über andere Berufswünsche und Erwartungen in beruflicher Hinsicht angeschlossen werden.

d   network support technician – research engineer – test engineer
electrical engineer – staff accountant – service technician
manufacturing engineer – sales representative

A Welcome to Leeds Airport!

b Schülerantworten

ⓘ *Bei dieser Aufgabe ist es empfehlenswert, die Vorgaben (Ausgangspunkt – Zielpunkt) vorzugeben. Die Schüler/innen werden dabei veranlasst den Lageplan genauer zu studieren. Außerdem sind dabei je nach Leistungsstand der Schüler/innen kürzere beziehungsweise längere Wege möglich.*

B Arrival at Power Engines Ltd

ⓚ **b** ❶ manufacturing, ❷ fuel engines, ❸ natural gases, ❹ bio-gases, ❺ hydrogen, ❻ boss, ❼ charge of, ❽ quality control

ⓚ **c** (Dialogvorschlag)

Introducing person:
"Dave, may I introduce you to Steven, our production manager."
Dave: "Nice to meet you, Steven."
Steven: "Nice to meet you. How was your train journey?"
Dave: "Oh, it wasn't too bad – there was just a delay of 10 minutes."

Introducing person:
"Mr. Delaney, this is Jane Owttrim. She is in charge of purchasing and stores at our company."
Mr Delaney: "How do you do?"
Ms Owttrim: "How do you do? I hope you didn't have any trouble finding the company."
Mr Delaney: "Well, actually I had no trouble at all. I just followed the excellent directions which were sent to me."

Introducing person:
"Ms Kahl, have you met Geoff Harris, our accountant here at Power Engines."
Ms Kahl: "Oh yes, we already met an hour ago."
Mr Harris "Nice to see you again, Ms Kahl. How was the weather in Munich, when you left?"
Ms Kahl: "It wasn't too good. – It was raining and it was a bit cold."

Introducing person:
"May I introduce you to Silke Meier. Silke is our public relations manager."
Helen Miller: "Nice to meet you, Silke. I understand you are in charge of public relations here."
Silke Meier: "Nice to meet you, Helen. Yes, that's right – and you work for the Manchester Observer."
Helen Miller: "Absolutely right. I must apologise for being late – but the traffic was terrible today."
Silke Meier: "Well, that's no problem – I was late myself."

Leistungsstärkere Schüler/innen sollten hier aufgefordert werden, einen freien Dialog anzuschließen, wie z.B. ein Interview zwischen Silke Meier und Helen Miller über die Aufgaben im Bereich Marketing der Firma. Allerdings benötigen die Dialogpartner einige Minuten zur Vorbereitung. Es empfiehlt sich die ersten drei Aufgaben zügig und ohne größere Vorbereitung durchzuführen. Bei der letzten Aufgabe werden gezielt stärkere Schüler/innen ausgewählt, die ein Interview im Anschluss an die Vorstellung durchspielen.

d Schülerantworten

e 1. How do you do?
2. I'm fine. (Thanks, I'm fine.)
3. Nice to meet you, too.
4. Nice to meet you.
5. Yes, thank you. (It was very calm/comfortable/nice.)
6. Well, that's okay. Never mind.

C Introducing the company

a Mögliche Antworten:

Emily Miller is David Shawn's secretary.
Bill Walker is in charge of personnel.
Steven Hill is responsible for production, engineering and quality control.
Peter Thompson reports to John Smiley, who is in charge of research and development.
…

b
- sales department
- purchasing
- quality control
- sales
- accounting
- advertising
- market research
- stores
- personnel
- research and development

c 1. museum
2. production area
3. canteen

d After leaving the testing facilities he must turn right and walk past the production area. At the first junction he has to turn left past research and development. At the end of the road he has to turn left again. From there it is straight on past the canteen and the administration building, which is on the right. At the end of the administration building Oliver can see the parking lot on the right.

(k) e The tour starts at the Visitors' Centre. The first destination is the administration building, where Emily Miller will meet them to give them a short introduction to Power Engines. Afterwards Emily will take them to the research centre. Here John Smiley, the head of Research and Development, will describe fuel-cell technology. Peter Thompson, John Smiley's assistant will then accompany them to the laboratories, where they hope to be able to watch an experiment.

D Grammar revision: Tenses

(k) a 1. was 2. have lived 3. went 4. studied 5. graduated 6. decided
7. am looking forward 8. have never worked and lived 9. have known
10. read 11. watch 12. am reading

(k) b 1. for 2. since 3. for 4. since 5. since 6. for

Unit 2
Office work

Diese Unit vermittelt im *Teil A* einen kurzen Überblick über einige einfache Bürotätigkeiten. Die Schüler/innen lernen die englischen Bezeichnungen für Büroutensilien und für einfache Vorgänge wie Ablage und Kopieren. Im *Teil B* geht es um Vokabeln und Redewendungen zum Telefonieren sowie um Buchstabiertabellen, Maße und Gewichte. In *Teil C* werden Standardbriefformen vorgestellt.

Das Niveau ist so gehalten, dass keine kaufmännischen Kenntnisse vorausgesetzt werden müssen. Wer einfache Bürotätigkeiten zu verrichten hat – sei es auch am heimischen Schreibtisch – kann bereits einen Gewinn aus dieser Unit ziehen.

Da die einzelnen Units des Grundkurses nicht streng aufeinander aufbauen, also auch selektiv bearbeitet werden können, müsste in den Fällen, in denen Unit 1 nicht vorher behandelt worden ist, die Person des Oliver Klein und die Firma Power Engines Ltd kurz erklärt werden (siehe Unit 1, Seite 7 im Schülerbuch). Im *Grammatikteil D* werden Adjektive, Adverbien und Präpositionen wiederholt.

Starter

a ❶ – clock ❷ – scissors ❸ – pencil sharpener ❹ – hole punch ❺ – biros (die Bezeichnung für den Behälter für die Kugelschreiber ist *desk tidy* oder *pencil caddy*) ❻ – stapler ❼ – notepad ❽ – tray ❾ – envelope ❿ – paper clips

b desks, chairs, shelves, a sideboard, a laptop, a desk lamp, flowers, a wastepaper basket, vases, a standard lamp, three pictures on the wall.

Für fortgeschrittenere Schüler/innen wären Antworten denkbar wie: The picture shows a very modern office: there are desks made of steel frames and glass; in the corner there is a conference table with four chairs.

A Office routine

a *Nach dem ersten Vorlesen durch die Lehrerin/den Lehrer mögliche Verständnisfragen:*
Why is Jane asking Oliver if he has seen Mike?
What does Oliver offer to do for her?
For whom does Jane need copies?
Where should Oliver put the copies?

Die Antworten können in Stichworten an die Tafel geschrieben werden. Nachlesen durch Schüler/innen in Dialogform.

Vertiefende Übung für fortgeschrittene Schüler/innen:
Schüler/innen sprechen den Dialog frei (oder mit Hilfe des TA – siehe oben) nach. Hierbei ist nicht der genaue Wortlaut des Originaltextes sondern die sprachlich richtige Wiedergabe des Inhalts wichtig.

(k) **b** 2, 4, 6, 1, 3, 5

(i) *Vertiefende Übung: Describe in your own words how you make photocopies on the machine at school, on a pay machine in the copy shop / post office etc.*

(k) **c** ❶ – purchasing   ❹ – communicate
   ❷ – familiar   ❺ – photocopier
   ❸ – suppliers   ❻ – make

(k) **d** 1. During the first week, Oliver will learn a bit of the routine in an office; he will find out how to make copies, he will learn important facts about his company's suppliers and he will learn how people in modern companies can communicate.

   2. Jane wants him to make four copies of the offer – one copy is for her files, the other three copies are for other people in the company: one for Steven Hill, one for his assistant, and one for Alan Brown.

   3. He puts the copies into each employee's pigeonhole.

(k) **e** *Vorschlag:* Our photocopier at school is a black-and-white copier. It is very simple to operate. All you have to do is put the paper face down on the glass screen, close the lid, press the button for the number of copies needed and then press the green print button. If you have two pages to be copied you can choose the "duplicate" mode to have two single pages copied on one sheet of paper, front and back. It can also sort the copies. It can use two paper formats, DIN A4 and DIN A3. Actually, it isn't very fast; it can do only two copies per second. The quality is not so wonderful, but it is o.k. for printed texts. One copy costs 5 cents, which is still quite cheap if you compare it with the price in a copy shop.

(i) *Für schwächere Schüler/innen kann der Lösungsvorschlag auch als Lückentext aufbereitet und kopiert werden.*

(k) **f** *Die Begriffe "incoming mail" und "outgoing mail" dürften den Schüler/innen bekannt sein, sofern sie schon mit E-Mail-Programmen gearbeitet haben. Die hier erwähnten Briefformen enquiry, offer, order – Anfrage, Angebot, Bestellung – sind die Standardtypen des Geschäftsbriefes* (siehe Unit 2, C).

(k) **g** (Lösungsvorschlag)
   For my private filing system I use five folders that are labelled as follows:

   1. Monthly Expenses – where I file my electricity and water bills, the receipts for my rent paid.

2. Insurance – here I keep my policies for car insurance or health insurance.
3. Private Letters – I don't have many letters in there, mostly letters to my parents and printouts of e-mails.
4. Important Documents – for documents such as my birth certificate, marriage certificate, contracts like the lease for my apartment, and my employment contract.
5. The school folder has everything in it that I need for school. This folder is the heaviest, because it contains not only my reports and classroom tests, but also important notes and tables for technology.
My problem is that I do not always file my papers correctly, so very often I have to search for them. I really should do my filing regularly once a week.

h *Hinweis: Das deutsche Wort „bitte" bereitet Schüler/innen immer wieder Probleme. Deshalb empfiehlt es sich, auf den Unterschied zwischen dem auffordernden „bitte" (please) und „bitte" in „wie bitte"? (I beg your pardon? oder Could you please repeat the question? I am sorry, I couldn't quite follow) und der Antwort auf Danke (You're welcome) einzugehen.*

i *Grammatik (siehe auch S. 179 im Grammatikteil): Stellung der "adverbs of frequency".*
Vertiefende Übung unter Benutzung der genannten Adverbien:
What do you usually do on weekends: (get up late, have a nice breakfast, call my friends, work for school, go out for a walk, do sports, go out for an evening meal, watch television).

B Telephoning

a *Dieser Dialog wird beim ersten Anhören vielleicht nicht ganz verstanden. Die erste Frage zielt daher auch nur auf den Hauptgegenstand des Gesprächs. Es genügt zunächst eine Antwort wie "The main point is that Oliver receives / is receiving a new offer."*
Für schwächere Schüler/innen kann auch das Dialogtranskript (S. 192) aufgeschlagen werden.

b *Je nach Vorbildung der Schüler/innen sollte vor dem zweiten Anhören terms of delivery and payment – Liefer- und Zahlungsbedingungen – erklärt werden.*
Ebenfalls wichtig ist der Unterschied zwischen Mrs und Ms [miz]. Hinweis auf Buchstabiertafel unten auf S. 23.

Die Fragen 1–5 sollten vor dem Anhören kurz vorgelesen werden. Bei schwächeren Schüler/innen sollte der Dialog auch mehrmals vorgespielt werden. Evtl. muss Frage 4 (What do the caller and Oliver agree on?) erklärt werden.

Bei den Lösungen sollten in den Schülerantworten auch Stichworte akzeptiert werden, da dies der Bürorealität eher entspricht als die sonst im Englischunterricht geforderten ganzen Sätze.

(k) 1. Andrew Slate from Distel Electronics is calling

2. He wants to speak to Steven Hill.
3. The call is about a new offer that Distel wants to make to Power Engines. They have found new suppliers and that is why they can produce 15% cheaper.
4. It is agreed that Power Engines will send an answer no later than Tuesday, the 12th.
5. If Mr Slate is not in, Mr Hill should contact Ms Auburn.

(k) c Urgent Message

Dear Mr Hill,

I received an important call from Mr Slate of Distel Electronics on Friday. They have found new suppliers and can now offer our control panels cheaper – by 15%! They offer the same terms of payment and delivery. However, they need your answer by Tuesday the 12th at the latest. If you are not able to reach Mr Slate you should contact Ms Auburn.

(i) d *Hinweis auf z.T. unterschiedliche tables in Großbritannien und den USA. Eine kleine Hilfe für die Schüler/innen: schwierigere Namen an die Tafel schreiben. Vertiefende Übung: Immer mal wieder in den folgenden Unterrichtsstunden Wörter buchstabieren lassen oder Namen oder Begriffe für die Schüler/innen buchstabieren.*

e

(k) Mr Hill: Hello, Steven Hill here / Steven Hill speaking.
Oliver: Good morning, Mr. Hill. This is Oliver Klein speaking.
Mr Hill: Did you have a nice weekend, Oliver?
Oliver: **Yes thank you, Mr Hill. But there is something we should discuss.**
Mr Hill: Fine, what's on your mind, Oliver?
Oliver: **On Friday afternoon I had a phone call from Distel Electronics. I've sent you a memo. They are making a new offer, cheaper than …**
Mr Hill: A new offer, and cheaper you say? How much cheaper?
Oliver: **15%.**
Mr Hill: And how can they suddenly be cheaper?
Oliver: **They said they had found new suppliers.**
Mr. Hill: How much time do we have to decide on the new offer?
Oliver: **We have to answer by Tuesday the 12th.**
Mr Hill: Well thank you, Oliver, that certainly is good news for a Monday morning.

f 1. 01705 (area code), 9133407 (number)

2. 0046 (country code), 23 (area code), 4978 (number)

3. 0049 (country code), 5651 (area code), 567481 (number)

4. 001 (country code), 215 (area code), 3451985 (number), 3451930 (fax)

h *Weitere Übung mit Hilfe der conversion tables, Seite 246 ff.*
Beispiel: The atomic weight of aluminium is ...
6°C equals 42.8°F

j *Weitere Adressen, die die Schüler/innen nennen könnten wären die Homepage oder die E-Mail Adresse der Schule, des Betriebs, Adressen des Lieblingssenders der Schüler/innen, des jeweiligen Internet- oder Handyproviders, Adressen für Referatsthemen und Hausaufgaben, Sportvereine etc.*

k 1. 1 pint 5. 2 ounces
2. 10 inches 6. 50 yards
3. 3 quarts 7. 2 acres
4. 5 gallons 8. 100 miles

Für fortgeschrittene Schüler/innen wäre folgende Hörverständnisübung möglich: Listen to the following sentences. Write them down and give the metric equivalent of the following measurements.

1. The diameter of the monitor screen is 17 inches.
2. The speed limit in many states in the USA is 65 miles per hour.
3. Our car gets 15 miles to the gallon. (In USA und GB wird der Verbrauch von PKW in miles per gallon angegeben, nicht in Liter pro 100 km)
4. Planes fly at an altitude of 33,000 feet.
5. The oil reservoir of the old lathe held about 2 qt.
6. It uses roughly 1 fl oz per working hour.

C Letter writing

a 1. e-mail 3. memo (kurze informelle Notiz)
2. business letter 4. fax

Tipp für fortgeschrittene Schüler/innen / für Schüler/innen mit kaufmännischem Hintergrund: Die Briefbeispiele können auch inhaltlich erfasst werden.

b 1. reference 5. subject matter
2. date 6. body of the letter
3. inside address 7. complimentary close
4. salutation 8. enclosure

ⓘ *Die folgende Infobox sollte nur soweit behandelt werden, wie es der jeweilige Lehrplan vorschreibt. Allen Schüler/innen sollten jedoch die Form der Anrede, die Zeichensetzung und Großschreibung nach der Anrede und die von der Anrede abhängige Grußformel vermittelt werden.*
Der Betreff (subject line) steht nach der Anrede, es ist aber auch möglich, ihn ähnlich wie im Deutschen vor die Anrede zu setzen.

ⓚ **c (Lösungsvorschlag)**

PE – Power Engines Ltd	Combustion Drive
	Leeds
	Date

Jackson & Green
156 Albert Docks
Liverpool 15 P 5SN

Dear Sir or Madam

<u>Your special offer for oil pumps in the June edition of Technical Equipment</u>

We are a company that has long been on the market developing and manufacturing alternative fuel engines. We have read your special offer for oil pumps in the recent edition of Technical Equipment and we are interested in a quotation for 100 oil pumps as specified in your advertisement. Please quote your most favourable prices and your terms of delivery and payment. If your quotation meets our expectations we will order larger quantities in the near future.

We look forward to receiving your offer.

Yours faithfully

Jane Owttrim
Purchasing Manager

ⓘ *Tipp: Für schwächere Schüler/innen wäre die folgende Aufgabe zur Aufgabenstellung im Buch eine gute Hilfe:*
Write a business letter with the facts given on page 31 (top right corner). Use the phrases in your letter of enquiry and put them in the right order, but don't forget the address, the date and the reference.

Combustion Drive
Leeds

You may be aware that we are one of the leading manufacturers in the field.
- and quote your most favourable prices, terms of payment and terms of delivery.
We have seen your advertisement and your special offer in the June edition of Technical Equipment.

Yours faithfully,
P.E. Power Engines Ltd,
Jane Owttrim /Purchasing Manager
Please send us a trial offer for 100 pumps ...
If your delivery is to our satisfaction you may expect large orders from us in the future.

d ❶ – Commerce   ❺ – favourable
   ❷ – supplier   ❻ – delivery
   ❸ – offer   ❼ – payment
   ❹ – order   ❽ – hearing

e
KeySys
Membrane Switches
Wilhelm-Röntgen-Strasse 14
74722 Buchen / Odenw

Virex – Virussysteme
PO Box 4969
Trevose PA 19053
USA   date

Dear Sir or Madam

While visiting a business partner who was being attacked by a virus we saw your antivirus program in action. Please send us an offer for a licence for a network with 40 clients and differentiate between a 1-year licence and a 2-year licence. Please specify in your offer whether your program also protects against viruses from the Internet and via e-mail.

We look forward to hearing from you soon.

Yours faithfully *

* Heutzutage wird immer häufiger eine saloppere Schlussformel gewählt, z.B. "Yours sincerely", oder "With kind regards".

Unit 2

D Grammar revision: Adjectives/Adverbs/Prepositions

I Comparison of adjectives: Adjectives/Adverbs/Prepositions

(k)
1 – faster
2 – cheaper
3 – slower
4 – more expensive
5 – most expensive / the best
6 – easier
7 – best
8 – worst

II Adjective or adverb?

(k)
1. nearly
2. familiar
3. really
4. well
5. hard
6. late
7. lately
8. hardly
9. fast
10. remarkably
11. well
12. obviously

III Prepositions

(k)
1. with ... of
2. on
3. to
4. at
5. by

Unit 3
Information technologies – Electronic Communication

In dieser Unit geht es um die neuen Informationstechnologien, um Computer-Hardware und Software-Anwendungen. Es wird nur ein geringes Wissen vorausgesetzt. Im *Unitteil A* werden zunächst die Hardwarekomponenten vorgestellt: PC, Tastatur, Bildschirm. Ein Text gibt auch einen kurzen historischen Abriss über die Entwicklung des Computers. Unterschiedliche Anforderung an die PC-Ausstattung werden ebenso behandelt wie ein Anruf bei einer Hotline bei Installationsschwierigkeiten.
Im *Teil B* geht es um verschiedene Softwareanwendungen: Schreibprogramme, Tabellenkalkulation, CAD und Anwendungen in der industriellen Prozesssteuerung. Es werden keine speziellen Kenntnisse in solchen Programmen benötigt.
Teil C ist den Informationsmedien gewidmet – im Wesentlichen dem Internet und Multimediaanwendungen. *Teil D* wiederholt die Hilfsverben.

Starter

a Bei den Abbildungen handelt es sich um folgende Geräte *(von links nach rechts):*
 – printer (Drucker),
 – screen oder monitor (Bildschirm, genauer handelt es sich hier um einen Flachbildschirm: flat screen),
 – PC (der eigentliche Computer, von der Bauform her ein mini tower)
 – disks and CD-ROMs
 – keyboard (Tastatur, z.B. *key* heißt hier Taste)
 – mouse
 – DVD drive (DVD Laufwerk, für DVD-ROMs; DVD steht für *digital versatile disk.* DVD-ROMs sind Datenträger, ähnlich wie CD-ROMs, die aber noch mehr Daten speichern können, beispielsweise lassen sich komplette Spielfilme speichern)
 – scanner
 ganz unten links:
 – graphic tablet (Eingabegerät; mit dem Griffel lässt sich auf diesem Tablett sehr genau zeichnen, genauer als beispielsweise mit einer Maus)

Für schwächere Klassen empfiehlt es sich diese Begriffe vorzugeben.

b input devices (Eingabegeräte): keyboard, mouse, scanner, graphic tablet
 output devices (Ausgabegeräte): printer, monitor
 storage devices (Speichermedien, -geräte): disks, CD-ROMs, DVD drive

c 1 – i   5 – c   9 – g
  2 – f   6 – l   10 – k
  3 – a   7 – h   11 – j
  4 – b   8 – e   12 – d

ⓘ *Vorschlag zur Vertiefung: Schüler/innen definieren die Geräte mit eigenen Worten (bei geschlossenen Büchern):*
What is a joystick? / What do you use a joystick for?
What is the function of a hard drive?
What is the difference between memory and hard drive? (Memory can store data only temporarily, that is, while the computer is switched on, whereas the drive stores data permanently.)

ⓚ **d** Computers control machines.
Computers can help you when you need up-to-the-minute information.
Computers speed up paperwork / speed up communication.
Computers facilitate communication / paperwork.

A Hardware

ⓚ The physical components of a computer such as the mainboard and the hard drive or the monitor are called hardware.

A1 The keyboard – the most important input device

ⓚ **a** A – Page down   I – Backspace
B – End   J – Caps lock
C – Delete   K – Ctrl and Alt
D – Page up   L – Space bar
E – Home (auch Pos1)   M – Enter (auch „Return"-Taste genannt)
F – Insert   N – Tab
G – Arrow keys   0 – Shift
H – ESC

A2 The development of computers

ⓚ **a** ❶ – inventor   ❻ – Englishman
❷ – devices   ❼ – modern
❸ – century   ❽ – between
❹ – lessons   ❾ – engineers
❺ – mechanical calculating machines   ❿ – weighed

ⓚ **b** ENIAC

ⓘ **c** *Falls diese Aufgabe für die Schüler/innen zu schwierig sein sollte, könnte der folgende Lösungsvorschlag auch als Übung verwendet werden.*

ⓚ The first microcomputers were terribly expensive devices. They had slow processors (for example 086 Mhz or 286 Mhz). They had no hard disk. You had your operating program, your application and your data on the same floppy disk (5¼"). Then you had two floppy disk drives, one for your programes to work with and one to store your data on. The monitors were only in black and white.

A3 What type of computer do you need for your job?

a 433 Mhz computer, 8 GB hard disk, 64 MB memory, CD-ROM (k)

b 1. Denise wants to update her computer and she wants the shop assistant to tell her a bit about the latest hardware and software that is available. (k)

2. She has a 433 MHz computer with a hard disk drive capacity of 8 GB, 64 MB memory and a CD-ROM drive.

3. He thinks that her computer is too old and that he probably won't be able to update it.

4. Denise needs the computer for CAD, word processing and spreadsheet programs. She also needs an internet connection for her computer and she would like a scanner and a digital camera as well.

5. The shop assistant tells Denise that it is very important to have a fast computer, because the faster the computer is, the faster one gets information from the Internet.

6. The shop assistant proposes that he write down all of the components Denise needs for her computer, and he promises to work out a good price for her.

A4 Comparing hardware

a *Hinweis: es sind mehrere Lösungen möglich.* (k)
keyboard: 30 function keys, ergonomically designed
CPU (memory): RAM speed
printer: ink jet, print quality, 50-sheet paper tray
loudspeaker: 30Hz-20KHz response
monitor: flicker-free, high resolution

b *Hier sind je nach Quellenmaterial unterschiedliche Antworten möglich.* (i)

c (Vorschlag) To begin with, all models are equipped with modems, so they are all capable of connecting to the Internet. (k)
The first model advertised can handle almost any office task and is therefore the tool for home offices. It is equipped with an Ethernet card and 250 MB Zip drive and its central processing unit is able to operate at a speed of 1.4 GHz. Additionally, the package contains a laser printer and a 19" monitor and all applications you need to run a modern-day home office. The main advantage of model A over models B and C is that all of the hardware components are state-of-the-art, whereas the other two models contain only the standard equipment.

Model C is clearly for a private user. It contains only the standard software and hardware. Its working memory is smaller than that of model A and the hard disk drive has only roughly a third of the capacity model A provides. However, it still has some advantages over model A, such as a DVD drive and a colour printer. Most important of all, model C costs less than half of what you have to pay for model A, so it is a low-priced alternative to model A.

Model B, a notebook, is for professional users who travel a lot. It is the slowest of all three models, but it is much lighter and much more compact than the other two. Furthermore, model B's modem offers a socket to plug in your mobile if there is no normal phone connection at hand.

(k) **d** Model A is the sort of computer a software programmer or professional designer would buy.
Model B is intended for brokers or business men who travel a lot by train or plane, or who work in a place where there is not enough room for a desktop computer.

Model C is the model for the standard home user, the one who uses the computer for all sorts of things, like writing letters or playing computer games, but who does not need it for work.

A5 Troubleshooting: Problems with installing hardware

(k) **a** The help desk is very friendly to the customer even though the customer is very impatient at the beginning of the dialogue. She is very understanding. The help desk asks precise questions to find out about the problem. She treats the customer as one always should: as a very important person, as one who you should never make angry.

(k) **b** The customer has bought a computer game called "Invade and Take Over" version 3.0, second release. The game doesn't accept the default setting of his sound card. He can't hear the proper sound. He just has a screeching sound.

(k) **d** 1. Paper jam – open the lid of the tray and remove the jammed paper.

2. Printer doesn't work – check the plugs.

3. E-mail is returned – check for correct address: every dot is important.

4. Program cannot save file on disk – either disk is full or the write protection is enabled.

5. When you start your computer it says "No system disk" and stops – remove floppy disk and hit any key.

6. Your word processor cannot open a file – file is already opened or corrupted.

7. You cannot get access to the Internet – check if your modem is switched on and properly connected.

8. Your system program tells you that it cannot start a program – not enough memory, too many programs are already open.

9. You play a multimedia game and cannot hear the sound – reinstall your sound card.

10. Your computer cannot read from your CD-ROM drive – CD-ROM needs cleaning.

A6 Storage devices:
Floppy disk – Hard disk – CD-ROM – DVD

a (Übersetzungsvorschlag)

Dateien können auf der Festplatte gespeichert werden. *(Den alternativen Begriff gibt es im Deutschen nicht, er kann also auch nicht übersetzt werden.)* Festplatten bestehen aus einem Stapel von Metallscheiben in einem separaten Rahmen/Gehäuse im Computer. Ihre Speicherkapazität ist um vieles höher als die einer Diskette. Festplatten speichern und laden Daten von sich drehenden/rotierenden Platten.

Sie halten nicht ewig, und viele Menschen sind schon Zeuge geworden, wie Festplatten kaputt gegangen und Daten verloren gegangen sind/sind schon Zeugen von Festplattencrashs geworden, bei denen Daten verloren gegangen sind. Es ist deshalb notwendig, dass Sie Ihre Dateien auch auf anderen Medien speichern. Eines der gebräuchlichsten/verbreitetsten Medien, die verwendet werden, ist die Diskette. Sie hat eine Speicherkapazität von ungefähr 1,4 MB, was nicht viel ist, aber genug, um Dateien zu speichern, die mit einem Schreibprogramm erstellt worden sind. Technische Zeichnungen jedoch benötigen mehr Speicherplatz. Hier wäre ein Zip-Drive mit 100 MB oder 200 MB Speicherkapazität geeigneter. Ein Zip-Drive kann auch zur Datensicherung benutzt werden.
Noch mehr Speicherkapazität bietet eine CD-ROM; sie ist ein Speichermedium von 650 oder 750 MB. Das vielversprechendste Speichermedium für die Zukunft ist die digital versatile disk, kurz DVD. Sie hat eine enorme Speicherkapazität von bis zu 17 GB, genug um ganze Filme darauf abzuspeichern.

(k)

(k) b

Storage medium	storage space	price (if available)	use
hard drive or hard disk	2 GB	€ 300	store programs and files
floppy disk (3 1/2")	1.4 MB	price for a drive: € 25, for the floppy € 0.40	files, e.g. word processor
Zip-drive	up to 200 MB	€ 150 for the drive, € 15 for the disk	backup, store programs and files
CD-ROM	up to 800 MB	€ 50 for the drive, € 0.50 - € 1 for the CD-ROM	files, programs, pictures, drawings, music
DVD	17 GB	€ 75 for the drive, € 35 for an empty DVD	files, programs, films

B Software

(k) a 1. Software is a set of instructions that tells the hardware what to do.
2. There are two kinds of software: system software and application software.

(k) b 1. controls the computer's internal operations - s
2. translates the user's commands into computer language – a (but in some cases also s)
3. includes word processors, spreadsheet programs or database management - a
4. controls peripherals such as monitors or floppy disk drives - s

B1 Drawing pictures – CAD

(k) 1 aided (e)   7 parts (c)
2 technical (m)   8 printed (h)
3 complicated (a)   9 measurements (b)
4 models (i)   10 attachments (k)
5 possible (l)   11 versa (d)
6 angle (f)   12 people (g)

B2 Computers in industry – CAM and CIM

(k) a *CAD* means computer-aided design; in other words you use suitable software to create technical drawings.

CAM stands for computer-aided manufacturing. Here computers are used to control machines and robots.

CIM is the most advanced technique, computer-integrated manufacturing. Computers run whole business processes, from contacts with customers, to the production of goods ordered, to the shipment of these goods.

b *Diese Aufgabe sollte nur mit Schüler/innen durchgeführt werden, die tatsächlich schon Einblicke in die industrielle Fertigung erhalten haben und die über gute Englischkenntnisse verfügen. Für Schüler/innen ohne diese Vorkenntnisse lässt sich folgender Lösungsvorschlag auch als Übung durchführen.* (i)

Computers in Industry (k)

There is hardly any production process that is not assisted by computers. Take the big CNC centres, for example, lathes or milling centres that can produce whole engine blocks for the car industry within minutes. Someone has to write the programs for these machines (done on a computer) and to provide the correct set of tools and the material. But then everything is controlled by the machine's computer. It clamps the workpiece, chooses the right tools, changes the tools and turns the workpiece in every position that is necessary.

B3 Using a computer to write: A word processor – important features

a With a word processor you can easily edit a document. One important feature is the cut-and-paste function. It also has a spell checker that marks words that are misspelled. (k)

b
copy	– C. kopieren	search	– G. suchen
cut	– A. ausschneiden	number	– I. nummerieren
edit	– D. bearbeiten	retrieve	– K. wiederfinden
format	– E. formatieren	select	– L. markieren / auswählen
insert	– J. einfügen	undo	– H. rückgängig machen
paste	– J. einfügen	replace	– B. ersetzen
save as	– F. speichern unter		

(k)

c
Zeichen	– B. character	Befehl	– G. command
Zwischenablage	– C. temporary file	Schriftgrad	– I. font size
Datei	– A. file	Fußzeile	– J. footer
Symbol	– D. icon	Silbentrennung	– M. hyphenation
Ansicht	– E. view	Grafikwerkzeuge	– K. graphic tools
Fenster	– F. window	Kopfzeile	– L. header
Dialogfeld	– H. dialogue box	Rechtschreibeprüfung	– N. spell checker

(k)

Zusatzfrage: Name the 10 most important features from the many you have just read and matched (b and c). **Zusatz**

(k) **d** a 3   f 7
     b 6   g 8
     c 5   h 4
     d 1   i 10
     e 2   j 9

(k) **e** ① – processor   ⑤ – edit   ⑨ – drawings   ⑬ – thesaurus
      ② – paste   ⑥ – screen   ⑩ – text   ⑭ – fonts
      ③ – drag   ⑦ – print   ⑪ – spell checker ⑮ – feature
      ④ – typewriter ⑧ – pictures   ⑫ – corrects   ⑯ – homepage

B4 Spreadsheet programs

(k) 1976

B5 Organizer manual

(k) **a** ① double-clicking   ⑩ entry
       ② manually   ⑪ message
       ③ deleted   ⑫ search
       ④ copy   ⑬ view
       ⑤ options   ⑭ automatically
       ⑥ receive   ⑮ corrupted
       ⑦ button   ⑯ loaded
       ⑧ entered   ⑰ saying
       ⑨ save

(k) **b**
Student A: How do I uninstall the program?
Student B: That is very simple. You enter "setup" and click on "uninstall".
Student A: Will I lose my files if I deinstall the program?
Student B: Yes, but you can copy the data from the file called data into another file on your hard drive.
Student A: How can I create a new entry?
Student B: You open the main window and click on the icon "Create new entry". When you see a new window, you click on the button "Enable writing" and then you can put in day and month and the appointment you have on that particular day.
Student A: Is it possible to change an entry, say if the appointment changes?
Student B: Certainly, all you have to do is open the main window, click on "View an entry", and on "Enable writing", then change the entry, But don't forget to click on the "Save entry" button.
Student A: Can I delete an entry altogether?
Student B: Yes, it's the same main window. From there you go to "Delete an entry" and you just follow the instructions.

B6 Programs and applications

Moderne Textverarbeitungsprogramme sind fast Alleskönner. Deshalb sind hier auch z.T. andere Antworten denkbar. Gute Textverarbeitungsprogramme haben Zeichenfunktionen genauso integriert wie Tabellenkalkulation.

(i)

(k)

graphics program:
Adding colour and patterns to objects
Creating rectangles, squares or other shapes
Drawing and manipulating objects
Inverting a picture
Making an object larger or smaller
Rotating an image

word processor:
Automatic numbering of chapters and sections
Displaying information in the form of a table
Mail merging applications
Proofreading documents using a spell checker
Searching for and replacing words
Writing faxes
Writing reports

spreadsheet program:
Calculating interest rates
Changing the value of cells
Changing width and height of columns and rows
Formatting multiple columns of text
Producing line charts and pie graphs
Making out invoices

database:
Controlling all sorts of data
Keeping records of students
Storing information about customers

electronic mail:
Exchanging information with other computer users

C The Internet – Communication and information
Starter

ⓘ *Auch ohne dass eigens eine Aufgabe für den Starter formuliert wäre, lässt sich anhand der Grafik auf Seite 49 gut in das Internet und seine Möglichkeiten einführen.*

What can you do with the Internet?

– download music
– find out about timetables of trains and planes
– retrieve information on economic developments
– find out about books / order books
– make travel arrangements for your holiday
– shop
– trade stocks and shares

ⓘ **a** Hier müsste evtl. auf die korrekte englische Bezeichnung für Mobiltelefon oder auf Deutsch auch „Handy" hingewiesen werden. Obwohl „Handy" englisch klingt, ist es keine gebräuchliche Bezeichnung im Englischen. Mobiltelefon heißt im BE: *mobile phone*, oder kurz *mobile*, im AE *cellular phone* oder *cell phone*.

ⓚ means of communication: telephone, mobile phone, fax / fax machine, Internet, satellite

ⓚ **b** 1. Business people often use mobile phones on trips so they don't have to rely on public telephones.

2. Mobile phones are becoming more and more popular with young people.

3. Overseas calls usually go via satellites because they are faster than undersea cables.

4. For ordering spare parts engineers often use a fax or e-mail, because that way they can send an exact drawing of the part they need.

5. Postcards are still in use for sending traditional Christmas greetings.

C 1 Getting information

ⓚ **a** This picture shows exactly how I sometimes feel. It expresses fear of not being able to handle all the information that is being poured over us. Yes, of course, it exaggerates somewhat, but it is clear that it is hitting a nerve.

ⓚ **b** To find out about the date of my classroom test I would use my telephone because that's probably the fastest and most convenient way.
If I am interested in tomorrow's weather my best source is definitely the newspaper.

As for sports results I prefer TV because it is fast and reliable.
The radio is certainly a good choice if you are interested in the DAX or other stock exchange news because it is easy to access and also very fast and reliable.
For consumer reports about cameras or computer equipment I usually consult weekly magazines or a special interest magazine. They are independent – I would not totally trust the information brochures of companies.
If I want to find out something about the production of steel or the melting point of copper, it is surely a good idea to use the old fashioned 20-volume encyclopedia or a modern encyclopedia on CD-ROM. You may also find valuable information in specialised books or technical books on the subject. The fastest way to look up a word in English is in a dictionary in book form or on CD-ROM.
If I had a problem with my printer I would try to find help in the Internet, because there are probably many people out there who have had the same problem and are ready to share their solution with others.

c When working with technical texts in a foreign language you can use a technical dictionary either in book form or on a CD-ROM. Both forms are very reliable. The dictionary in book form can be used everywhere, on the train or comfortably in your armchair. In such cases the book has a clear advantage over the CD-ROM. For the CD-ROM you need your computer; you have to wait until it is ready.
As you know, the world of technology is constantly changing; new things are discovered. Naturally the vocabulary changes as well. Here the dictionary on CD-ROM has a clear advantage over the book. It can be updated within minutes. This is a definite plus.

(k)

Hier zwei weitere Beispiele, die vielleicht von fortgeschritteneren Klassen so gelöst werden könnten (die Texte sind auch geeignet als zusätzliche Übungstexte):

Zusatz

Television is certainly our number one source when it comes to both information and amusement. First of all, you have an unbelievable choice of stations and channels. There is hardly anything that you are not able to receive on television, be it hooked to cable or to a satellite. You have information and entertainment practically around the clock. So TV is always accessible and it certainly is up-to-date.
But at what price? You only have to pay fees for our public channels, private channels are free. The news is not always reliable and is often governed by the principle "only bad news is good news", because the majority of viewers are attracted by sensational news. And it is a fact that the private TV stations have to attract people – the more, the better – because they have to finance their programmes by selling time for advertising. Therefore, the films you want to watch are interrupted by commercials for soap or sodas.

The *newspaper* is a good source of information at a reasonable price. It comes out daily and informs you about regional matters as well as national or international events. You can read it on the bus or train on your way to work or while waiting at the doctor's office. You can keep your source of information in your pocket, so that it is available whenever you are ready for it. It may not be as up-to-date as TV or radio, but you can read the news that you may have heard on TV the night before at your own pace and receive more background information. For people who do not like to read, the newspaper seems a tedious medium – and maybe it is for people who are addicted to fast-moving "information" from news clips.

C2 Databases – Electronic Sources of Information

(k) **a** An encyclopedia in ten or twenty volumes has one clear advantage over an encyclopedia on CD-ROM: you can pull it out of your bookshelves whenever you need it. You do not have to switch on your computer or laptop. And you can lean back in your armchair with the book on your knees, which is not so easy to do with a computer.
Of course an encyclopedia with so many volumes is very expensive – the CD-ROM with the same amount of material on it is much cheaper. This is a definite plus, especially for students.
Another advantage of the CD-ROM over the encyclopedia in book form is that you can print out the material you have found. And in some cases you can even hear extracts of speeches that the person you are reading about once gave. Multimedia is not possible in book form.
Another disadvantage of the traditional encyclopedia is that you cannot update it; with a CD-ROM, you just connect your computer to the Internet and download additional data.

(i) **b** *Hinweis:* Diese Aufgabe bedarf einiger Vorbereitung. Einmal müssten die Schüler/innen Zugang zu den genannten Medien haben und zum anderen muss auch die Form der Präsentation abgesprochen und gegebenenfalls geübt werden. Als Präsentationsformen wären hier denkbar: Die Ergebnisse werden von Kleingruppen erarbeitet und mündlich präsentiert. Oder sie werden auf einer Folie der Klasse vorgestellt oder bei geübteren Schülerinnen und Schülern in Form einer Power Point -Präsentation.
Hinweis: theromosetting plastics sind Kunststoffe, die nach dem Erhitzen in eine Form gebracht werden, die sie auch bei nochmaligem Erhitzen nicht mehr verändern. Thermoplastische Kunststoffe dagegen können öfter erhitzt und in neue Formen gebracht werden – siehe Schülerbuch S. 108.
Hinweis: alloy bedeutet Legierung, siehe Schülerbuch S. 105.

C3 The Internet

Zusätzliche Übung als Einstieg: Zusatz

Folgender oder ein ähnlicher Fragebogen kann entweder von einer Gruppe in der Klasse entwickelt und ausgeteilt werden, oder aber er wird von der Lehrerin / dem Lehrer gleich ausgeteilt, bearbeitet und dann ausgewertet (u. U. wieder von einer Gruppe).

Questionnaire: How do you use the Internet?

Have you got access to the Internet?

How often do you use the Internet?
- more than once daily
- daily
- every other day
- once a week
- less than once a week

What kind of services do you use? Check off three of the services that are most useful to you.
- e-mail
- read the news
- find out about sports results
- check consumer reports
- log into chat groups
- get information on your hobbies
- get information on subjects important for your job

a The Internet was invented in 1969 when the American defence system wanted to create a global network to make sure that the information between, let's say point A and B, could be exchanged not only through one channel (that could easily be interrupted) but through two or three channels. Later, other government institutions and universities were also admitted to this network. Another important invention took place in the year 1989 – the invention of a common protocol for the exchange of information between clients and servers. The inventor's name is Tim Berners-Lee. (k)

b *Diese Aufgabe ist nur mündlich zu lösen.* (i)

c *Hier bieten sich Fragen nach der Preisstruktur an, nach den gegenwärtigen Modetrends und technischen Neuerungen. Es ist anzunehmen, dass sich in jeder Klasse Schüler/innen finden, die über solche Neuerungen gut Bescheid wissen und die Mitschüler, aber auch die Lehrer/innen informieren können.* (i)

C4 Internet addresses

(k)
1 – f   6 – k
2 – g   7 – c
3 – a   8 – e
4 – h   9 – b
5 – i   10 – d

C6 The Internet – some legal aspects

(k) **a** One danger, always present, is that somebody might check your own computer while you are online. People may spy on you, or steal data from you. The text does not mention, however, the danger of a virus attacking your system while you are online. Planting and distributing viruses is an illegal act and is punishable by law. The chances of detecting the person who invented or wrote the virus program and sent it off into the net are very high, because every user of the net leaves traces.

(k) **b** The most important precaution is having a virus protector installed. Secondly, you should never leave your computer alone while you are online, so nobody can invade your system. You should give your credit card number only to on-line shops or institutions you know and trust.
After having done bank business never surf on the Internet, because the passwords used are still in your system and can be detected. The best thing would be not to have any personal data on the computer you use for the net, or to have two separate computers, one with your personal stuff on it and one for surfing the internet.

C7 Information management

(i) **a** *Diese Aufgabe ist nur für Schüler/innen geeignet, die tatsächlich schon Erfahrungen mit dem Suchen und Herunterladen von Daten haben. Geeignete Maßnahmen zusätzlich zu der im Text genannten wären z.B. eine genaue Vorbereitung einer online-Sitzung (was wird gesucht, welche alternativen Stichworte gibt es), Speichern der heruntergeladenen Datei in einem gesonderten Verzeichnis, das regelmäßig gesichtet und gelöscht wird. Nur relevante Daten sollen behalten werden.*

C8 The Internet language

(k) *modem, net, tool, domain, surfer, link, chatbox, USB, website, download, hypertext*

C9 Mulitmedia

a Multimedia programs combine text, pictures, sound and video sequences. Often they also offer interactive components; that means the user can determine which steps the program has to take next.   (k)

b The text describes certain computer games as forerunners of multimedia where the player was able to decide which path the characters of a game should take. Then the text discusses language programs that make use of multimedia and interactive applications. The third example of multimedia is presentations by companies for their customers and shareholders.   (k)

c *Hier wären Fragen denkbar nach der Art der Programme und vor allem Fragen nach den unterschiedlichen Multimedia-Anwendungen.*   (i)

D Grammar revision: Auxiliaries

a   1 – can   7 – must not   (k)
     2 – must   8 – must not
     3 – must not   9 – must
     4 – need not   10 – can
     5 – should not   11 – can
     6 – should   12 – cannot

b   1. … he will have to contact   (k)
     2. … they were able to help
     3. … you were allowed to test
     4. … we did not have to
     5. … had to be reorganised

Unit 4
Mechanical engineering – Tools

(i) Diese Unit soll neben der Vermittlung berufsbezogener englischer Sprachfertigkeiten der Fachrichtung Maschinenbau auch dazu dienen, der Sprachlehrerin/dem Sprachlehrer die Scheu vor dem fachtechnischen Hintergrund zu nehmen, d.h. es soll deutlich gemacht werden, dass kein Ingenieurstudium in Maschinenbau notwendig ist, um in diesem Bereich Englisch zu unterrichten.

Als Einleitung werden einige der gebräuchlichsten Handwerkzeuge, Elektrowerkzeuge und Werkzeugmaschinen kurz vorgestellt. Bei der Begehung der Lehrwerkstätten der virtuellen Firma DEP in *Teil A* lernen die Schüler/innen die Ausstattung einer Grundwerkstatt kennen, wobei die Postitions-Bindewörter (next to, in front of, etc) wiederholt werden.
Als nächstes werden die im Maschinenbau üblichen Verbindungs- bzw. Montagetechniken behandelt, sowohl mechanischer Art mit Bolzen, Schraub- u. Nietverbindungen als auch durch Schweiß- u. Klebeverbindungen.
Im *B-Teil* geht es um die wichtigsten Werkzeugmaschinen (machine tools) wie Dreh- Fräs- u. Schleifmaschine (lathe, milling machine, grinding machine) und deren wichtigste Bauteile und Funktionen. Am Beispiel der Elektrobohrmaschine wird die Gruppe der Elektrowerkzeuge behandelt, auf die in Unit 5 nochmals detailliert eingegangen wird.
Bei all diesen Inhalten wird besonderer Wert auf die berufliche Kommunikation gelegt (Funktionsbeschreibungen, Bedienungsanleitungen, Verkaufsgespräch). Das Gleiche gilt für das wichtige Thema der Sicherheit am Arbeitsplatz in *Teil C*.
Im *Grammatikteil D* werden Fragesatzkonstruktionen und Relativsätze (notwendige/nicht notwendige) mittels situativer berufsbezogener Übungen wiederholt. Zusätzliche Übungen und Arbeitsblätter als Kopiervorlage werden im Anhang angeboten.

Starter

(k) **a**
1. screwdrivers (k)
2. combination pliers (j)
3. spanner (e)
4. set of Allen keys (c)
5. lathe (g)
6. vice (a)
7. hacksaw (b)
8. handsaw (i)
9. electric drill (h)
10. adjustable wrench (d)
11. riveting tongs (f)
12. toolbox (l)

(i) *Bei leistungsstärkeren Schülerinnen/Schülern:*

1. *zusätzliche Zuordnungsaufgaben ohne "list of tools"*
2. *Nennen der Werkzeuge im Werkzeugkasten*
3. *Ergänzung durch weitere Handwerkzeuge, Elektrowerkzeuge und Werkzeugmaschinen*

b 1. machine tools: lathe
2. power tools: electric drill
3. hand tools: screwdrivers, combination pliers, spanner, set of Allen keys, vice, hacksaw, handsaw, riveting tongs, adjustable wrench, toolbox

c *Diese Übung eignet sich auch als Dialogform, z.B. stellt die Schülerin/ der Schüler die/der die Antwort gibt die nächste Frage. Bei leistungsstärkeren Schüler/innen kann diese Übung ohne "word box" gemacht werden.*

1. tightening or loosening
2. drill/bore
3. work
4. clamp
5. work
6. drive in
7. screwing
8. cut
9. cutting
10. drilling; mark

A Shop floors and joining methods
A1 Visiting the shop floor of a machine tool company

a It's the workshop shown on page 58.
Reasons:
- two column drills between the large windows
- a centre lathe next to the blue door
- a milling machine opposite the lathe
- the men's washroom is the first door on the right just before you leave the workshop.

b To the right of the (bench) vice there are two screwdrivers.
On top of the workbenches next to the column drill there are vices (there is a vice on each)
Between the workbenches there is a column drill.
In front of the (bench) vice (next to the lathe) there is a hammer.
Behind the lathe there are two screwdrivers.
Between the lathe and the column drill there is a vice.
To the right of the column drill there is a workbench with a vice on top.

Für leistungsstärkere Schüler/innen ließe sich diese Übung ergänzen durch Beschreibung der auf S.58 und S.59 abgebildeten Werkstatteinrichtungen (workshop equipment/facilities).

c ❶ the shop floor
❷ a chief executive
❸ Industries Fair
❹ apprentices
❺ a centre lathe
❻ manufacturing centre
❼ a spindle
❽ skilled workers
❾ milling machine

Unit 4

(i) *Tipp: Für leistungsschwächere Schüler/innen könnten die Begriffe in der "word box" durch die deutschen Bedeutungen ergänzt werden.*

A2 Joining

(k) **a** The joining methods mentioned in the text are: riveting (techniques) – welding and soldering – bonding with adhesives.
Other joining methods are: nailing – screwing. The tools to be used are a hammer, screwdrivers, spanners, nails, screws, bolts and nuts.

(i) **b** *Diese Übung eignet sich eher für leistungsstärkere Schüler/innen, bei denen auf eine differenzierte Einleitung der Sätze durch die entsprechenden Bindewörter zu achten ist. Bei leistungsschwächeren Schülerinnen/ Schülern kann auf diese Differenzierung verzichtet werden.*

    A: First, I've got to assemble these two base plates of a machine vice.
    B: Well, you'll need socket screws and nuts.
    A: And after that I need to tighten the bolts of the machine vice.
    B: I suppose you'll need a spanner and an Allen key, won't you?
    A: Next, I need to weld the two pieces of sheet metal over there.
    B: I wouldn't weld them, because the material is aluminium. I'd rather rivet them. The box of rivets and riveting tongs are over there on my workbench.
    A: And before we can take our coffee break, these two flat steel plates must be joined to form a square.
    B: Well, now you have to weld of course. You can use my welding torch, but be careful when you're handling the welding equipment.
    A: By the way, I'm afraid I broke the handle of the coffee pot in our office. Have you got some adhesive?
    B: Yes, I have. There's a new tube of mixed adhesive in the top drawer of my desk.

(k) **c** Student A: I've got to join two metal bars.
    Student B: Why don't you weld them?
    A: I want to bond these two broken ceramic parts.
    B: You'll need some adhesive.
    A: I've got to tighten these nuts and bolts.
    B: You'll need a spanner.
    A: I want to join two wooden boards.
    B: Why don't you nail them together?
    A: I've got to join these two sheets of metal.
    B: You'll need some riveting tongs.
    A: I've got to solder these copper wires.
    B: You'll need a soldering iron.

B Machine tools and power tools
B1 Machine tools

Hintergrundinformation: Bei den folgenden drei Werkzeugmaschinen – Drehmaschine (lathe; centre lathe; turning machine), Fräsmaschine (milling machine) und Schleifmaschine (grinding machine) – handelt es sich um Maschinen, die zur Grundausstattung einer Ausbildungwerkstatt und Produktionswerkstatt im Maschinenbau (mechanical engineering) gehören. Sie werden eingesetzt für sog. spanabhebende Bearbeitungsverfahren (cutting processes), weil hierbei grundsätzlich mit Schneide- oder Schnittwerkzeugen (cutting tools) Material in Form von Spänen (chips) abgehoben wird. Diese drei Maschinentypen unterscheiden sich im Wesentlichen wie folgt:

Mit der Drehmaschine werden runde Teile hergestellt (turning machine); die Arbeitsschritte haben also mit Drehbewegungen (revolutions) zu tun.

Mit der Fräsmaschine werden flache, rechtwinklige oder winklige Teile hergestellt. Die Bewegung des Werkzeugs verläuft immer in gradliniger Richtung, und zwar entweder horizontal (horizontal milling machine) oder vertikal (vertical milling machine).

Mit der Schleifmaschine werden Materialoberflächen mit hoher Genauigkeit bearbeitet und geglättet. Die Bewegungen der Schleifwerkzeuge (grinding tools/discs) können sowohl rund als auch gradlinig ausgeführt werden (cylindrical grinding; flat grinding).

Für genauere automatisierte Arbeiten mit hoher Produktionsstückzahl werden CNC (Computerized Numeric Control)-gesteuerte Maschinen im CIM (Computerized Integrated Manufacturing)-Verfahren eingesetzt.

Es empfiehlt sich für Sprachlehrer/innen, die von der fachlichen Materie nur geringe Kenntnis besitzen, sich von Fachkollegen in den Werkstätten informieren zu lassen. Sehr anschaulich und handlungsorientiert lässt sich dieser Themenkreis auch mit Schülergruppen in den Werkstätten bearbeiten, wobei die Schüler/innen aus den technischen Fachrichtungen i.d.R. gern ihre fachliche Hilfe anbieten. Allerdings sollte hier die Lehrerin/der Lehrer allzu fachspezifische Expertendiskussionen so steuern, dass der fremdsprachliche Aspekt wieder in den Mittelpunkt der Betrachtung rückt.

(k) a base table   Grundtisch
      bed/frame   Rahmen/Gestell
      base   Sockel/Bett
      centre lathe   Drehmaschine
      chuck   Spannfutter
      column   Ständer/Säule
      emergency stop   Notschalter
      grinding machine   Schleifmaschine
      grinding wheel   Schleifscheibe
      headstock   Spindelkasten
      knee   Winkeltisch
      main switch/push button Hauptschalter
      milling machine   Fräsmaschine
      overarm   Führungsarm
      saddle and cross-slide (Unter-) Schlitten/Support mit Querschlitten
      table   Maschinentisch
      tailstock   Reitstock
      toolpost   Werkzeughalter/Stahlhalter
      table traverse   beweglicher Schleiftisch
      vertical slide   Senkrechtschlitten

(k) b **lathe:**   **milling machine:**   **grinding machine:**
      – bed/frame   – base   – base
      – base   – column   – base table
      – chuck   – emergency stop   – column
      – emergency stop   – knee   – emergency stop
      – headstock   – main switch/push button   – grinding wheel
      – main switch/push button – overarm   – main switch/
      – saddle and cross-slide   – table   push button
      – tailstock   – vertical slide   – table traverse
      – toolpost

Zusatzaufgaben: Siehe Arbeitsblätter auf S. 106/107.

B2 Centre lathe

(k) a A: Where exactly is the   B: It's at the left top end of the lathe.
         headstock?
         ... the emergency off?   ... on the top right-hand side of the
                                             control panel.
         ... the tailstock?   ... at the right top end of the lathe.
         ... main switch?   ... usually at the left end of the machine.
         ... chuck?   ... on the nose of the main spindle.
         ... toolpost?   ... on top of the saddle and cross-slide.

b *Dieses Gruppengespräch ließe sich mit leistungsstärkeren Schülerinnen/ Schülern anhand der Zeichnungen oder auch vor Ort in den Werkstätten erweitern bzw. als Gruppenpräsentationsübung gestalten.* ⓘ

ⓚ

A: What's the function of the chuck?
B: Well, it holds the cutting tool during the turning operation.
C: I'm afraid that's not quite right. The function of the chuck is to hold the workpiece during the whole turning operation
A: What's the function of the machine bed?
B: It supports the saddle and cross-slide and the toolpost during the operation.
C: Yes, that's right.
A: What is the saddle and cross-slide needed for?
B: Well, it holds the cutting tool during the turning operation.
C: That's not quite right. It's the toolpost that holds the tool during the turning operation. It seems to me that the main function of the saddle and cross-slide is to provide the feed for longitudinal turning of the cutting tool.
A: What's the toolpost needed for?
B: It holds the workpiece during the whole turning operation.
C: I don't agree here. The toolpost holds the cutting tool during the turning operation.

Als Ergänzung könnte man als Hilfe für leistungsschwächere Schüler/innen diese Funktionserklärungen von leistungsstärkeren Schülerinnen/Schülern auf Deutsch interpretieren lassen (nicht übersetzen), womit gleichzeitig das unterschiedliche Leistungsgefälle etwas sozialisiert würde. ⓘ

c motor: – The motor powers/drives the spindle, the gears and the automatic slides. ⓚ

gear and control unit: – With the gear and control unit you can set the different speeds of the spindle and control the different feeds.

emergency switch: – In case of emergency you can stop the complete machine immediately with this switch.

main switch: – The main switch provides the machine with electric power.

motor-reversing switch: – With the motor reversing switch you can set the rotation of the spindle either clockwise or counter-/anticlockwise.

speed-selection lever: – The speed-selection lever is necessary to set the rotation speed of the spindle.

B3 Milling machine

(k) a 1. motor
       2. vertical slide
       3. overarm
       4. start-and-stop switch
       5. table

    b 1. elements (3/20)
       2. anticlockwise (26)
       3. toolpost (23)
       4. mounted (29)
       5. cutting tool (19/28)
       6. provides (10)
       7. workpiece (19/25)
       8. feed(s) (18)

(i) c *Die Schüler/innen sollten hier immer ganze Sätze formulieren, z.B. The knee carries...*

(k)
knee	E	column	C
base	D	overarm	G
table handwheel	B	table	H
start-and-stop switch	A	spindle	F

B4 Grinding machine

(k) 1. **The cross-feed handwheel** provides the table cross-travel.
    2. **The base table** stores grinding wheels.
    3. **The table** carries the desired workpiece to the grinding wheel.
    4. **The main switch** controls the electrical supply to the machine (on/off).
    5. **The grinding wheel** removes the material from the workpiece.
    6. **The table traverse handwheel** provides the longitudinal table movement.

B5 Power Tools

(k) a 800.1.6   is an impact drill
       800.2.8   is an angle grinder
       800.56.7 is a cordless (light-duty) drill/screwdriver drill

(i) *Ergänzungsübung: Suche und Bestimmung von weiteren "tools", "power tools" und "machine tools" im Internet.*

(k) b **impact drill** – Standard equipment: chuck key, side handle and depth gauge
    – Variable pre-selection of speed for optimum drilling results
    – 2-speed power tool, ideal for DIY, professional, automotive and industrial use

    cordless drill – 48 external torque settings for precise settings of screws
    – New battery technology for maximum runtime
    – Reversible drive with adjustable torque settings, screwdriver bits, spanner and adapter

angle grinder — Supplied complete with grinding disc and handgrip
— A compact powerful tool, ideal for general grinding jobs in the garage, workshop at home
— Ideal for sanding large panels
— Compact power tool, ideal for sanding car bodies.

c **Discount Tool Store:** — batteries – screwdrivers – wrenches
Cordless Tools: — battery-driven impact drills
Bits: — drill bits
Safety and Protection: — gloves – goggles
Storage of Tools: — a box for your tools
Woodworking Mac.: — chainsaws – band saws

d 1. a drill; a cordless screwdriver drill; screwdriver bits; spanners
2. a sander; an angle grinder
3. stripping tongs; screwdrivers
4. an impact drill; a carbide-tipped drill; a cordless screwdriver drill; screwdriver bits
5. a welding torch
6. a hacksaw
7. a sander with an abrasive disc
8. a file

f These are the features of the cordless screwdriver drill:
— it's reversible (umschaltbar)
— it has a two-speed variable trigger switch (Zwei-Gang-Umschalter)
— there are five torque adjustments (Drehmomenteinstellungen)
— there are two 9.6-V DC battery cartridges rechargeable in 1 hour (9V Akkus mit einer Ladedauer von 1 Stunde)
— their service life is more than 2 hours of operation (2 Stunden Betriebsdauer)
— it has a red signal light to indicate low charge (rote Signallampe zum Anzeigen von Niedrigspannung)
— there's a 1-hour quick charger with an auto shut-off (Schnellladegerät mit 1 Stunde Ladedauer)
— there's a safety lock out of the power when not in use (Sicherheitsabschaltung bei Nichtbetrieb)
— the material of the case is 100% recyclable (wiederverwertbar)

g — Powerful 650 watt motor — Kraftvoller 650 Watt Motor
— Safety clutch — Sicherheitskupplung
— Synchromesh two-speed gear — Synchronisiertes Zweigang-Getriebe
— Adjustable auxiliary handle with integral depth gauge — Verstellbarer Zusatzhandgriff mit integriertem Tiefenanschlag
— Compact ergonomic design — Ergonomisches Gehäusedesign
— Fully insulated metal gearbox — Vollisolierter Metallschaltgetriebe

Unit 4

– Clockwise/anticlockwise rotation	Recht-Links-Lauf
– Optimal on-load speed for drilling up to 24mm	Optimale Lastdrehzahl für Bohrdurchmesser bis 24mm
– Hammer stop	Schlagstop
– Keyless chuck for tightening without a key	Schnellspannbohrfutter für werkzeugloses Spannen

(i) **h** *Leistungsschwächere Schüler/innen könnten hier ein Wörterbuch zu Hilfe nehmen.*

(k)
A: Hello, can I help you?
B: Hello. I'm looking for a power tool for drilling.
A: What do you need it for?
B: I'd like to set up a few shelves in my new flat.
A: Are the walls concrete or brick?
B: Concrete.
A: Well, in that case I'd recommend an impact drill/hammer drill. This is our latest model.
B: What features does the device have?
A: First of all it has got a powerful 1000 watt motor and a synchromesh two-speed gear.
B: Has the model also got a clockwise/anticlockwise rotation?
A: Yes, certainly. Furthermore, the device has got a hammer stop and a safety clutch.
B: What about the tool exchange? Can it be done quickly?
A: Yes, the new model comes with a keyless chuck for tightening drills and screwdriver bits.
B: Is it also possible to drill holes with a diameter of 20mm?
A: Yes, the machine drills holes up to 24mm in diameter. By the way, the handling is made a lot easier by the reliable/tried and tested adjustable auxiliary handle with depth gauge.
B: Oh, yes, I know this already from the previous model. Oh, before I forget, do you trade in old drilling machines for new ones?
A: Of course/That goes without saying, just as offered in our advertisement.

(i) **i** *Hier bleibt es der Lehrerin/dem Lehrer überlassen, welche Elektrowerkzeuge beschrieben werden sollen. Die Schüler/innen könnten auch Gebrauchsanweisungen aus ihrem praktischen Alltag zum Vergleich heranziehen.*

(k) **j**
1. Put the battery cartridge into the 1-hour charger.
2. Set the trigger switch for low speed.
3. Adjust the required torque for this drilling operation.
4. Select the direction of rotation with the reversing lever.
5. Replace the discharged battery with a recharged one.
6. Read the required revolution speed off this table.
7. Put the plug of the charger into that socket over there.
8. Reset the rotation for clockwise direction.

C Safety regulations in a workshop

a
I. Prohibition signs: 10 – 12 – 14 – 16
II. Warning signs: 2 – 6 – 17 – 19
III. Mandatory signs: 7 – 9 – 11 – 15
IV. Emergency signs: 1 – 3 – 5
V. Fire safety signs: 4 – 8 – 13 – 18

(k)

b
I. Prohibition signs: 7
II. Warning signs: 3 – 4 – 9 – 10
III. Mandatory signs: 1 – 6 – 8 – 9
IV. Emergency signs: 2 – 5

(k)

Als Ergänzungsübung könnten leistungsstärkere Schüler/innen die Unterschiede zwischen den deutschen und den englischen Sicherheitstafeln herausarbeiten, z.B.: "All English warning signs show the word DANGER written in white on a red background."

(i)

c
– gloves   1
– goggles   4
– hard hat   2
– ear protection   5
– fire extinguisher 9
– guard   6
– welding mask   8
– safety boots   3
– emergency off   7

(k)

Als Ergänzungsübung könnten leistungsstärkere Schüler/innen die Funktion der in c dargestellten Sicherheits- und Schutzausrüstung beschreiben, z.B.: "Goggles protect the eyes against chips produced during cutting processes at machine tools."

(i)

d
1. Avoid **loose clothing**. (h)
2. If you have long hair, don't forget to wear **a hair net**. (f)
3. Wear **a mask or a handshield** when welding. (k)
4. Don't forget to wear your **safety boots**. (i)
5. Position the **guards** of your machine tool correctly. (b)
6. Wear **gloves** when you work with sheets of metal or glass. (c)
7. Switch off the **mains** in case of emergency. (d)
8. Put on your **goggles** before you start grinding. (e)
9. Take care that **escape routes and emergency exits are not blocked**. (g)
10. Take care that the **fire extinguisher** is always in good working order. (a)
11. Watch out for **slippery oil** on the floor of the gangways. (l)
12. Read all **safety rules** carefully. (j)

(k)

e Student A: I'm going to stop work for today.
   Student B: Don't forget to return all tools after use.

   A: I need to bring in a new column drill.
   B: Keep the gangways free for transport.
   A: I'm going to drill some holes in the plate.
   B: Don't forget to wear a hair net.
   A: I'm going to grind the surface of the metal block
   B: Don't forget to wear goggles.
   A: I need to carry heavy metal stock into the milling shop.
   B: Don't forget to wear safety boots.
   A: I'm going to weld two bars.
   B: Wear a mask or a handshield.
   A: I need to repair the cable of the hammer drill.
   B: Watch the defective insulation.

D Grammar revision: Questions and relative clauses

I. 1. example
    2. example
    3. Where did Herr Braun show his visitor to?
    4. Why do the apprentices get some basic training at the machine tools?
    5. What can you see opposite the centre lathes?
    6. When will the metal-cutting machines be set up?
    7. How can these tools be used?
    8. What does the motor provide the power for?
    9. What is the headstock supported by in vertical machining centres?
    10. Where must the workpieces be clamped?

II. 1. The factory often has visitors from abroad, who are required to wear hard hats during the tour.
    2. The apprentices, who are presently working at a milling machine, are doing their first year of training.
    3. The table supports the machine vice, which clamps the workpiece in the required position.
    4. Joe, who is one of DEP's skilled workers, needs some help with his work.
    5. The lathe tool, which can be used for various turning jobs, must be sharpened for the facing operation.
    6. Our latest lathe model, which we demonstrated at the Hanover Fair, is equipped with a high-speed spindle.

Unit 5
Troubleshooting, maintenance and warranties

Im Umgang mit Werkzeugmaschinen und Elektrowerkzeugen kommt es oft zu Betriebsstörungen. Also ist es wichtig zu wissen, was die Fehlerquellen oder Störungsursachen sind. Dies wird in *Teil A* exemplarisch an einer Ständerbohrmaschine (column drill) gezeigt. Für den Heimwerker ist diese Information unter anderem in den Bedienungsanleitungen (manuals) zu finden. Hierzu gibt es entsprechende Übungen in *Teil B*. Im Arbeitsalltag eines Metallberuflers oder bei Heimwerkerarbeiten (DIY jobs) wird deshalb auch der Wartung (maintenance) und im Schadens- bzw. Reparaturfall den Garantiebestimmungen (warranties) der Hersteller besondere Aufmerksamkeit geschenkt. *Teil C* bietet hierzu reichlich Übungen und Aufgaben, wobei wiederum der Sicherheitsaspekt für den Fall der Fehlersuche und -behebung (troubleshooting) beachtet werden muss.
Im *Grammatikteil D* wird die indirekte Rede (reported speech), die indirekte Frage (reported question) und der indirekte Befehl (reported command) anhand von situativen berufsbezogenen Übungen trainiert.

Starter

a 1. The battery is low.
2. The keyless chuck is blocked.
3. The twist drill is blunt/broken/loose.
4. The trigger switch is set anti-clockwise.
5. The electric motor is damaged.

b

Student A	Student B
A: What's wrong with the twist drill?	**B:** It's blunt and must be sharpened.
A: Why isn't the twist drill properly clamped?	**B:** Because the keyless chuck is blocked.
A: What's wrong with the electric motor?	**B:** It's damaged and must be repaired.
A: Why doesn't the drill make a proper hole?	**B:** Because the switch is set anti-clockwise.

c *Die folgenden Lösungen sind nur ein Vorschlag, d.h. diese Übung kann natürlich je nach Bedarf erweitert werden. Siehe die „Prompts" im Textbuch.*

Student A:

A: The power drill is out of order. Do you know what's wrong with it?
A: Sorry, the twist drill doesn't seem to be working properly, could you check it, please?
A: I can't get the machine tool to work. Could you take a look at the power supply?

Student B:

B: Maybe the battery is low.
B: It looks like the drill is broken.
B: Let's have a look at the electric lead. It looks like the plug has come loose.

A Troubleshooting – A column drill

(i) *Es empfiehlt sich, diesen Lektions- und Übungsteil am Objekt Ständer/ Tischbohrmaschine fachtechnisch gut vorzubereiten, um das Ordnen des Dialogs zu erleichtern.*
Bei leistungsschwächeren Schülerinnen und Schülern kann auf Anordnung der korrekten Dialogreihenfolge verzichtet werden. Ihnen könnte nach Anhören des Dialogs dieser als Kopie vorgelegt werden.

(k) Dave Crewe: What's the problem, Steve? Any trouble with the machine?
Steve Pearson: Yes, it's not working and I don't know why.

Dave: Did you check the main switch?
Steve: Yes, of course I did. That was the first check, and I checked the safety button as well.
Dave: Well, let's see. Look here, Steve, the safety button is still locked in, you see? To release it, you must turn it a bit to the right and then pull it out, okay?
Steve: All right. And could you please check if the machine is set correctly?
Dave: Hmm, the spindle's set fine and the drill's properly clamped in the chuck. But what about the revolution speed?
Steve: Well, as the drill is an HSS centre drill I set the speed as high as possible, which is 2,500 revolutions/minute.
Dave: Fine, and you know that after centring you read the required revolution speed from the table here at the front of the machine gear box?
Steve: Yes, I know. The diagram in the table tells you the ratio of revolution speed and diameter of the drill.
Dave: And think of the machine table. It should be set high enough for you to drill properly into the material.
Steve: Oh yes, you're right, thank you. And the machine vice must be in central position as well?
Dave: Yes, you've got it. If you have any more problems, just give me a ring.
Steve: Will do. And thanks again!

B DIY Power Tools Manual

Als Anschauungsmaterial ließen sich für diesen Lektions- und Aufgabenteil leicht ein paar der erwähnten Bohrertypen präsentieren.

a drill bit   Bohrer
   twist drill   Spiralbohrer
   tungsten-carbide drill Hartmetallbohrer
   multi-purpose drill   Mehrzweckbohrer
   diameter *   Durchmesser
   HSS   Hochleistungsstahl
   versatile   vielseitig
   brad   Zentrierspitze

   * oft in der Kurzform "dia" verwendet

b 1. first   4. now
   2. then   5. finally
   3. after that

Mit leistungsstärkeren Schülerinnen und Schülern könnte man den Text "Tips on drilling" ganz oder teilweise ins Deutsche übersetzen.

C Maintenance and warranty

C1 Maintenance of a power drill

a *1. cleanliness*
   Example: Ventilation slots must be kept clear.
   – Collected dust should be removed regularly from the chuck.
   – Open and close the chuck completely. The collected dust will fall from the chuck.
   – Take drill out from time to time to remove dust.

   2. care
   Example: Hold the machine vertically with the chuck facing down.
   – Regular use of cleaner spray for the clamping jaws and jaw borings is recommended.
   – Contact one of STAR TOOLS' service agents when non-described components need to be replaced.
   – Switch to impact drilling for concrete, hard bricks, stone, hard cement, and marble.
   – Use bits with carbide tips.
   – Always hold sheet metal firmly in a vice.
   – Lay block of wood under thin metal to prevent it from distorting.
   – Use HSS drill bits.
   – For lubrication use oil for steel, turpentine or paraffin for aluminium.

- Don't lubricate when drilling brass, copper, cast iron.
- Take drill out frequently to cool it off.
- Use screwdriver bits of appropriate size and shape.
- Pre-drill into hardwood and for screws of large diameter or countersunk screws.
- Use bit reception to loosen screws in anti-clockwise operation.

3. *spare parts*
Example: Use only original parts.
- Accessories with part numbers in catalogue.
- CD-ROM with 1500 exploded views and 100,000 data sets.

Zusatz *Vereinfachte Aufgabe für leistungsschwächere Schüler:*

Find more information in the text that fits into the categories
1. cleanliness
2. care
3. spare parts as listed below.

1. cleanliness
- open and close the chuck completely. The collected dust will fall from the chuck
- take drill out from time to time to remove dust

2. care
- contact one of STAR TOOLS' service agents when non-described components need to be replaced
- switch to impact drilling for concrete, hard bricks, stone, hard cement, and marble
- lay block of wood under thin metal to prevent it from distorting
- use HSS drill bits
- for lubrication use oil for steel, turpentine or paraffin for aluminium
- don't lubricate when drilling brass, copper, cast iron
- use screwdriver bits of appropriate size and shape
- use bit reception to loosen screws in anti-clockwise operation

3. spare parts
- CD-ROM with 1500 exploded views and 100,000 data sets

(k) Key:
1. cleanliness – collected dust should be removed regularly from the chuck
2. care – regular use of cleaner spray for the clamping jaws and jaw borings is recommended
   - use bits with carbide tips
   - always hold sheet metal firmly in a vice
   - take drill out frequently to cool it off
   - pre-drill into hardwood, for screws of large diameter, countersunk screws
3. spare parts - accessories with part numbers in catalogue

b A 3. Changing the keyless drill   D 5. Setting the depth gauge   (k)
    B 4. Inserting tools   E 6. Selecting impact drilling
    C 2. Positioning the auxiliary handle   F 1. Selecting forward/reverse drive

c 1. **A** When should the collected dust be removed from the chuck?   (k)
     B When the machine is used for impact drilling.

   2. **A** What has to be done to remove the dust completely?
     B The machine must be held with the chuck facing down vertically, and the chuck has to be opened and closed completely.

   3. **A** How can the clamping jaws and the clamping jaw borings be maintained?
     B They must be cleaned regularly with a cleaner spray.

   4. **A** What do you recommend for finding accessories and spare parts?
     B Check our catalogue or CD-ROM.

   5. **A** What sort of drills should be used for masonry jobs?
     B Use percussion carbide-tipped masonry drill bits and don't forget to switch to impact drilling before you start working.

   6. **A** Why is it better to lay a block of wood under thin metal?
     B This way the metal won't distort.

   7. **A** What sort of drills must be used for metal work?
     B Use HSS spiral drill bits.

   8. **A** What lubricants are used for drilling brass, copper, or cast iron?
     B No lubricants are needed, but the drill should be taken out of the hole frequently to cool off.

   9. **A** Can this tool be used for screwing?
     B Yes, of course, but use screwdriver bits of the appropriate size and shape.

   10. **A** Can this tool be set anti-clockwise for loosening screws?
     B Yes, certainly, but in anti-clockwise operation the bit reception should be used.

Zusatz

C2 Warranty

a *Leistungsstärkere Schüler/innen können hier die Falschaussagen korrigieren.*   (i)

   1. false – TOOLPRO gives a one-year warranty.   (k)
   2. true
   3. false – You can claim warranty only if you are the original purchaser.
   4. true
   5. false – The warranty does not cover damage which occurs in service by anyone other than an authorized TOOLPRO Service Center.

(k) **b** Bill Morris von DEP ruft bei STAR TOOLS an und reklamiert den Elektro-bohrer STAR 600 SP, weil der Links-Rechts-Lauf nicht mehr funktioniert. Er teilt mit, dass er den Bohrer vor vier Monaten gekauft habe, woraufhin ihm zugesichert wird, dass das Werkzeug noch in die sechsmonatige Garantiezeit fällt. STAR TOOL Service schlägt ihm vor, die Bohrmaschine zusammen mit der Garantiebescheinigung und der Kaufquittung zu einem Vertragsservicedienst zu bringen, wo sie repariert oder ersetzt wird. Eine Liste der Servicedienste stehe auf der letzten Seite der Gebrauchs-anweisung.

(k) **c** 1. power drill   4. defect
    2. reversing switch 5. servicing
    3. warranty

(k) **d**

Student A	Student B
Hello, this is STAR TOOLS. Can I help you?	Hello, this is Bill Morris from DEP. We've got some trouble with your power drill STAR 600 SP.
What seems to be the problem?	It's the reversing switch which is sticking.
I see. When did you buy the tool?	About three months ago. Can we claim the warranty?
Yes, of course. We give a 1-year warranty on all our products.	Ah, that's fine. What do I have to do then?
Just send the tool to an authorised service centre. You'll find a list of our service centers at the back of your manual.	Oh, fine. Thank you for your help. Goodbye.
You're welcome. Goodbye.	

(k) **e Safety instructions**

Scrabble:

1. VIA
2. HARMFUL
3. GOGGLES
4. GLOVES
5. REMOVE
6. USE
7. OFF
8. MAINS (LEAD)
9. DRILLS
10. AVOID

A	S	Q	V	D	K	P	S
B	A	O	L	R	F	X	H
G	V	I	A	I	R	U	A
G	O	G	G	L	E	S	R
L	I	K	K	L	M	E	M
O	D	L	M	S	O	F	F
V	O	J	A	M	V	R	U
E	S	M	I	L	E	N	L
S	J	U	N	P	L	U	G
N	M	L	S	M	P	M	D

D Grammar revision: Reported speech

1. The instructor told Mike to open and close the chuck completely when cleaning dust out of it.
2. Matt reminded Phil and Sarah not to forget to clean the jaws and jaw borings with cleaner spray.
3. The instructor advised the trainee to use percussion carbide-tipped bits for masonry drilling.
4. He also told him not to forget to switch to percussion drilling before he started working.
5. Kate reminded Mark to use HSS spiral drill bits for metal work.
6. The trainee told his colleague to use turpentine or paraffin as lubricants when drilling aluminium.
7. The instructor told the trainee to use screwdriver bits of the appropriate size and shape.
8. He also advised him to pre-drill hardwood and when using countersunk screws.
9. Bill asked Steve whether he had set the switch anti-clockwise.
10. Dave said that he would meet the service engineer at the entrance.
11. Steve promised (that) the drill would be repaired the next day.
12. The instructor complained that he'd been waiting for 2 hours.
13. The instructor asked the trainee if he had checked the insulation of the mains the day before.
14. Dave said (that) the machine wasn't working and (that) he didn't know why.
15. Dave asked Steve if he had clamped the twist drill properly.
16. Dave wanted to know why the drill didn't make a proper hole.
17. Dave said (that) he had released the safety button.
18. The trainee told the instructor (that) the component hadn't been finished yet.

Unit 6
Electrical engineering

ⓘ Im *A-Teil* werden zunächst die Grundlagen der Elektrotechnik auf einfache und verständliche Art dargestellt. Die wichtigsten Werkzeuge des Elektrikers werden vorgestellt. *Troubleshooting* und das Kapitel Sicherheit beim Umgang mit elektrischen Materialien runden den Teil A der Unit 6 ab.

Der *B-* und *C-Teil* beschäftigt sich mit der angewandten Elektrizität: von der Batterie über den Elektromotor bis hin zur modernen Brennstoffzelle, die derzeit in der Forschung als mögliche Lösung der Energiefragen des 21. Jahrhunderts diskutiert wird.

Passive Sprachformen bilden die Grundlage von technischen Beschreibungen. Die Wiederholung der *Passive Voice* steht daher im Mittelpunkt der *Grammar Revision* in dieser Unit.

Starter

ⓘ **a** *Bei dieser Übung sollen die Schüler/innen lediglich ihre Vermutungen zum Ausdruck bringen – die eigentlichen Lösungen sind im Hörverständnistext zu erhalten. Zunächst sollen die Schüler/innen nur rein spekulativ vorgehen.*

ⓚ **b**
dishwasher	432 kWh/year	mobile phone	20 kWh/year
refrigerator	642 kWh/year	water heater	2190 kWh/year
TV	292 kWh/year	microwave	89 kWh/year
vacuum cleaner	38 kWh/year		

ⓚ **c**
hairdryer	9,31	electric heater	10,34
printer (stand by)	0,87	10 electric bulbs	223,38
printer (in use)	0,25		

ⓘ **d** *Bei dieser Übung bietet es sich bei schwächeren Klassen an, die gebräuchlichsten Formen des Vergleichs im Englischen vorab im Tafelanschrieb festzuhalten.*

z.B. ausgehend vom Deutschen:

genauso ... wie	nicht so ... wie	mehr ...als / weniger ... als
as ... as	not as ... as	more ... than / less ... than

ⓚ An electric heater consumes as much energy as a vacuum cleaner.
A printer doesn't consume as much energy as an electric bulb.
A TV consumes less energy than an electric heater.
A TV consumes more energy than a printer.
The energy consumption of an electric bulb is higher than that of a printer.
The energy consumption of an electric bulb is lower than the consumption of a hair dryer.

A Some basic facts about electricity
A1 General information

Die Schüler/innen sollen erkennen, dass uns statische Elektrizität im Alltag ständig begegnet. Nach der Klärung des Begriffs sollen sie Beispiele aus ihrem täglichen Leben geben, bei denen sie mit statischer Elektrizität in Berührung kommen.

A2 Batteries (chemical energy)

Eine wesentlich wichtigere Rolle spielen Batterien, die Strom in Form von chemischen Vorgängen freisetzen. Die Schüler/innen erkennen, dass diese chemischen Vorgänge einsetzbar sind, um kleinere Mengen von Strom zu erzeugen. Elektronen fließen vom negativen zum positiven Pol. Bei diesem Vorgang entsteht Strom, der beispielsweise in einer Taschenlampenbatterie nutzbar wird.

A3 Generators (mechanical energy)

Auf mechanischem Weg wird Strom mit Hilfe des Magnetismus erzeugt. Mit Hilfe eines Generators wird eine elektromagnetische Induktion hervorgerufen, die einen Strom erzeugt. Dieser Strom wird einem äußeren Kreislauf zugeführt. Auf diese Weise kann sowohl Gleich- als auch Wechselstrom erzeugt werden.

a Static electricity does not move. It builds up with friction and is suddenly discharged. Current is the electricity which is produced by moving electrons. This can happen via a chemical reaction or mechanically, with the help of electromagnetism.

b Unlike charges attract each other; like charges repel each other.

c Generators work according to the principle of magnetism. They turn movement into electricity. This principle is called electromagnetic induction. Electricity is produced in a wire when it moves in a magnetic field. The movement can be given by steam, moving water, or wind. In a generator a conductor moves through a magnetic field. The current which is produced is directed to an external circuit.

d
1. current
2. repel
3. generated
4. ammonium chloride
5. 1.5 volts
6. dissolve
7. applied
8. atoms

A4 Electrostatic induction

(k) 1. ❶ tap
❷ repel
❸ attract

2. ❹ jumper
❺ opposite
❻ move
❼ friction
❽ neutral
❾ hang

A5 Direct Current (DC) and Alternating Current (AC)

(k) a Der elektrische Strom, der durch eine Batterie erzeugt wird, ist Gleichstrom. Hier fließen die Elektronen nur in eine Richtung, d.h. vom negativen (Kathode) zum positiven (Anode) Pol.
Die Stromversorgung besteht jedoch nicht aus Gleichstrom, sondern aus Wechselstrom. In diesem Fall bewegen sich die Elektronen 50 mal in der Sekunde hin und her. Die Frequenz des Wechselstroms wird in Hertz (Hz) gemessen.
Die Pole der Stromversorgung wechseln ständig von Positiv zu Negativ und umgekehrt, was für den Verbraucher am Ende der Leitung keinen Unterschied macht. Eine Glühbirne leuchtet egal in welcher Richtung der Strom fließt

(k) b 1. generated   4. customer
2. to and fro   5. when the current flows in either direction
3. repeatedly

(k) c
• circuit	A continuous path of conductors and other electrical components along which an electrical current can flow.
• voltage	The unit of measure of electrical force.
• watts	Power is measured in watts.
• amps	When a battery is connected to a circuit, it produces an electric current. This current is measured in amps.
• direct current	Electric current flowing only in one direction.
• resistor	A resistor restricts the flow of current.
• coulomb	The unit of measurement of an electric charge.
• electric circuit	The path for an electric current.
• insulator	A material that does not conduct electricity.
• current	The amount of flow of electricity is called current.
• ohms	The resistance is measured in ohms.
• conductor	A substance that allows the passage of electrons.
• alternating current	Electric current that changes direction continuously.

A 6 Tools for electricians

a
- Abisolierzange — wire strippers
- Phasenprüfer — neon screwdriver (mains tester)
- Kneifzange — pincers
- Kombizange — combination pliers
- Schraubendreher — screwdrivers
- Flachrundzange — round-nose pliers
- Seitenschneider mit Handschutz — diagonal cutting nipper with hand guard

b Neon screwdrivers are used for testing electric current.
You use pincers to cut electric wire.
Combination pliers can be used for various tasks. For example, you can use them instead of wire strippers to strip electric wires.
Screwdrivers are necessary when you have to tighten or loosen wall sockets.
Round-nose pliers are very useful when you want to pull out a wire.
A multimeter is necessary for checking the flow of electricity.
If you want to cut a live wire, you have to use a diagonal cutting nipper with hand guard.

A 7 Troubleshooting

1. Example
2. First of all I would check the water softener. Next I'd see if salt had to be put into the appliance.
3. I would first check the electricity supply. Then I'd try to find out if the water supply had been interrupted.
4. In this case I would check the spray arms. They might be blocked by small items or remains of food.
5. First of all I would check the water supply. It might be that the water tap is not turned on. Next I would control the appliance door. Perhaps it's not properly closed. Finally I'd check the plug.
6. I'd check if the water softener was set too low.

A 8 Electricity and safety

a Do not remove the casing from an electrical device!
Do not use any damaged cables!
Don't dispose of empty batteries in the dust bin!
Never touch live electric wires!
Switch off the mains before working on electrical equipment!
Never replace bulbs with wet hands!
Never use a hair dryer in the bath tub!

Never use the flex/cable to pull the plug out of the socket!
Don't use indoor electrical appliances outdoors!

(k) c –In an electric accident, I would first switch off the electric supply. Then I would remove the victim from the danger zone. If the patient were in shock, I would place him in the shock position.

–If the respiration and the pulse of the patient were normal, I would still place the patient in the side position. I would ask the patient to remain calm until the doctor arrives.

B Electricity applied
B 1 The car battery

(k) a 1. If cells are connected in parallel the voltage of the battery does not increase, but the amperage will be higher.

2. The total voltage of parallel-connected cells depends on the number of cells which are connected in series. In car batteries you normally have six cells, which produce 12 volts.

3. In car batteries the cells are connected in series. Most cars have a 12-volt battery containing six 2-volt lead-acid cells. Plates of lead dioxide and lead metal immersed in sulphuric acid generate electricity.

4. Lead-acid cells can be recharged. This process takes place as soon as the engine begins to run. Lead sulphate, which is formed during the discharging process, is reversed into lead dioxide and lead metal during the recharging process.

(k) b You can increase the voltage of a battery by connecting the individual cells in series.

(k) c 1. number   5. contain
      2. depend   6. sulphuric
      3. connect   7. chemical
      4. alternatively   8. rechargeable

B 2 The electric motor

(k) a Individuelle Lösungen durch die Schüler/innen. Z.b.: electric toothbrush, electric fan, electric toy cars.

(k) b As far as the advantages and disadvantages of electric cars are concerned the most important positive aspect in my opinion is the lack of pollution. Electric cars are not only environmentally friendly but also absolutely quiet. On the other hand, there are certain disadvantages we should not ignore. Electric cars are limited in their range. Consequently, recharging becomes a problem, especially as there are not enough recharging stations. Furthermore, electric cars are heavier than regular cars because of the bulky batteries necessary for storing the electricity. In addition, these batteries are very expensive. To sum up: From my point of view the electric car is no alternative at the moment but may well be one day, when the technology is more sophisticated.

c Electric motors are absolutely clean. They do not produce any pollutants. From an environmental aspect they are very promising. We use electric motors for many purposes, such as to drive lawn mowers or electric chain saws or for running machinery in a workshop. In order to run an electric motor a source of energy is necessary. We normally use the mains as the source. The AC current of the mains is converted into a DC current. A kind of generator within the device produces the necessary power to run the motor.

d 1. external source of energy   5. coil
   2. direct current   6. commutator
   3. mains   7. electric current
   4. direct current motor   8. attractive force

C New technologies: Hydrogen and the fuel cell
C 1 The fuel of the 21st century: Hydrogen

a Wasserstoff als Energieträger einzusetzen erhält in diesen Tagen neuen Auftrieb. Obgleich Wasserstoff das am häufigsten vorkommende Element auf der Erde ist, stellt die Gewinnung von reinem Wasserstoff die Menschheit vor gewaltige Probleme. Aufgrund der geringen Konzentration von Wasserstoff in der Atmosphäre muss er aus wasserstoffhaltigen Stoffen unter Anwendung verschiedener chemischer Verfahren gewonnen werden.

Reiner Wasserstoff kann prinzipiell auf zwei Arten als Energieträger eingesetzt werden. Einerseits auf eine recht traditionelle Weise, indem Wasserstoff in einem Verbrennungsmotor als Treibstoff eingesetzt wird; andererseits kann Wasserstoff zur direkten Gewinnung von Strom verwendet werden. Mit Hilfe der Brennstoffzelle gelingt es, Strom ohne negative Begleiterscheinungen für die Umwelt zu erzeugen.

Die ersten mit dieser Technologie betriebenen Fahrzeuge sind als Prototypen bereits im Einsatz. Eines der Hauptprobleme im Zusammenhang mit dieser neuen Technologie stellt die Infrastruktur und Versorgung im Zusammenhang mit Wasserstoff dar. Die Technologie auf Basis der Brennstoffzelle wird jedoch als zukunftsträchtig angesehen, zumal nur wenige oder gar keine schädlichen Emissionen entstehen.

b *Die Präsentation der Schüler/innen kann – insbesondere bei leistungsstarken Klassen und falls die technischen Voraussetzungen dazu vorliegen – mit Hilfe von Präsentationsprogrammen am Computer vorbereitet und danach mit Beamer vor der Klasse präsentiert werden. Diese Übung eignet sich besonders für selbstorganisierte Lernformen. So können beispielsweise im Internet Informationen zur Brennstofftechnologie und Bilder bzw. Filmsequenzen herunter geladen werden. Aber auch andere Formen der Präsentation wie beispielsweise Folien sind durchaus denkbar, insbesondere wenn die technischen Voraussetzungen nicht vorhanden sind.*

Mögliche Antworten sind:

(k) 1. Hydrogen is chemically extracted from hydrogen-rich materials. It can be produced from natural gas using a method called steam reforming or from water by electrolysis.

2. In space technology hydrogen is used for propulsion and as an on-board source of energy.

3. In transportation hydrogen can be used in three ways. First, pure hydrogen can be used as a fuel in internal combustion engines. Second, with the help of fuel-cell technology, hydrogen generates electricity in a direct way.
And last but not least, hydrogen can be added to traditional fuels in order to reduce pollution.

4. In a fuel cell pure hydrogen is used to generate electricity in a direct way. The technology is comparable to the technology of a battery. In this process electrons and protons are set free and travel to a cathode, thereby producing electricity.

5. Fuel cells do not produce any harmful pollutants.

6. The main problems at the moment concern the infrastructure: There are not enough refuelling stations or garages for service and maintenance. Another major obstacle could be the price of such cars.

7. ZEVs are cars which do not pollute the environment at all.

(k)   c   1. technology   4. emission
              2. electrolysis   5. combustion
              3. electricity   6. efficiency

(k)   d   1. in recent years   6. conventional
              2. unlike   7. preferable
              3. abundant   8. furthermore
              4. present   9. urban
              5. major   10. lack

C2 Power Engines' fuel cell system

a 1. Internal combustion engines burn fuel to create heat, which is then converted into mechanical energy. The efficiency is rather low. A lot of energy is lost by wasted heat and friction.

2. The fuel cell is more efficient because there is a direct conversion of energy into power.

3. Another positive side effect of fuel cells is the fact that no harmful emissions are produced by this process.

4. Batteries have to be recharged, while cars using the fuel-cell technology only have to be refuelled.

b *Denkbar ist hier ein Gespräch zwischen zwei Schülern, die jeweils eine gegensätzliche Meinung zur Thematik vertreten. Die Gegner und Befürworter erhalten einige Minuten Zeit, um Argumente für das Streitgespräch zu sammeln. Danach wird der Dialog vor dem Plenum vorgespielt.*

c *Ausgehend von Meta-Suchmaschinen lässt sich unter dem Stichwort 'fuel-cell' reichlich Material zum Thema erschließen. Ein weiterer Tipp sind die Homepages von großen Automobilfirmen, die nahezu alle auf dem Gebiet der Brennstoffzelle forschen und ihre Ergebnisse ins Internet stellen.*

Diese Übung eignet sich im Rahmen von SOL (selbstorganisiertem Lernen) zur Präsentation vor dem Plenum. Je nach den technischen Möglichkeiten an der Schule kann die Präsentation mit Hilfe von Computer und Beamer dem Plenum vorgestellt werden.

D Grammar revision: Passive Voice

a 1. has been stored
2. was needed
3. was added
4. are mostly equipped
5. being developed

b 1. All the components are placed in front of you.
2. The combination pliers are used to cut the electric wire into three pieces of equal length.
3. The insulation of the wires is stripped off at the end.
4. Two pieces of the electric wire are connected to the socket of the lamp.
5. The switch is connected at one open end of the electric wire.
6. The other spare wire is connected to the switch as shown in the picture.
7. The bulb is put into the socket.
8. The switch must be turned off.
9. The open end of the wires is fixed to the battery.
10. The power supply is switched on.

Unit 7
Properties of materials and quality standards (ISO)
Starter

(i) Im *Teil A* dieser Unit geht es um die Beschreibung von Materialien und Formen. *Teil B* thematisiert die Eigenschaften von unterschiedlichen Materialien, wie sie in diversen Fertigungsprozessen verwendet werden: Metalle, Legierungen, Nichtmetalle, keramische Stoffe und Kunststoffe. *Teil C* vermittelt einen Einblick in den Bereich der Messgeräte, der Qualitätsstandards und des Qualitätsmanagements. Im *Grammatikteil D* wird das *gerund* wiederholt.

(i) • *Die Aufgabe ist je nach Vorbildung der Klasse zu lösen. Es ist nicht notwendig, dass die Schüler/innen zu jedem der genannten Materialien ein Fahrzeugteil nennen können, vielmehr sollen sie durch den Starter für das Thema Materialien und deren Eigenschaften sensibilisiert werden.*

Lösungsvorschläge:

(k)
- Copper is used for the electrical parts of the generator because it is a good conductor of electricity.
- Ceramics are used in some engine parts, particularly for spark plugs, because they do not conduct electricity. They are also used for brake discs.
- Plastics and fibreglass are used for the bumpers and the dashboard, because they are easy to keep clean and they are flexible instead of brittle, making them less dangerous in case of an accident.
- Fuel tanks are made of plastic with the advantage that the container is seamless, and fuel lines are partly of plastic because of its flexibility.
- Steel is used for the car body, as it is very strong.
- Aluminium is used for the wheel rims, as it is very light and rust resistant. Because of its thermal conductivity, aluminium is also used for air-conditioning systems, radiators and oil coolers.
- Cast iron is used for parts of the engine casing.
- Wood is sometimes used for the gear-shift knob in luxury cars.

A Describing products
A1 Which material for which design?

(k) **a** wood, steel, chromium, glass, leather, aluminium

(k) **b** wood: classic, easy to work with, strong and sturdy, lasts long, repairable, burnable
steel: elegant, more durable than wood, formable, shiny
chromium: nothing mentioned
glass: nothing mentioned
leather: nothing mentioned
aluminium: soft, light, resists corrosion, can't be painted

c *Lösungsbeispiel:*

We designed a desk tidy consisting of two oval, concave glass plates. It rests on four steel feet, and the two plates are also connected by four feet. We use special glue to connect all the parts. We decided on glass and steel because they go well with modern office equipment. Glass can be dusted and kept clean easily. And you can easily see what is in it.

d *Lösungsbeispiel:*

The overhead projector consists of two parts: the cubic housing with the glass projection screen for the transparency on top and the arm that carries the small casing for the lens and the mirror.

In the cubic housing are the transformer and the fan, and under the glass plate is the projecting lamp. On the top of the housing, front end, you have the main switch and two other switches, one for the regular lamp and one for a substitute lamp in case the main lamp is broken. From the rear end of the housing the red lead cable emerges; it is red so that teacher and students can easily see the cable on the floor and not trip over it. The glass plate on the top of the housing is square and milky white.

The reflector mirror is attached to the arm that itself is fastened to the casing. Next to the small casing for the mirror is a handwheel that helps you to adjust the mirror for accurate focusing. The mirror itself can be moved up or down, so that you can focus it onto the projecting screen on the wall.

e 1 square
    2 triangle
    3 circle
    4 oval/ellipse
    5 polygon
    6 pyramid
    7 cube
    8 cylinder
    9 rectangle
    10 diameter
    11 radius

f sketch

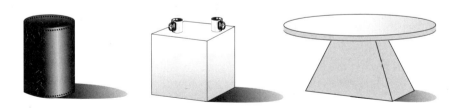

B Engineering materials
B1 Materials – an overview

(i) *Es gibt außer der hier vorgenommenen Einteilung der Materialien in bestimmte Stoffgruppen auch andere. Sofern in den Technologiebüchern (z.B. Metalltechnik) der Schüler/innen unterschiedliche Tabellen/Einteilungen verwendet werden, könnten sie diese im Englischunterricht vorstellen.*

(k) a leather   non-metals, natural materials
       gold   metals, non-ferrous; heavy metals
       silver   metals, non-ferrous; heavy metals
       mild steel metals, ferrous
       titanium   metals, non-ferrous

(k) b ① wood or stone   ⑨ porcelain
       ② copper   ⑩ temperatures
       ③ ferrous   ⑪ sintered
       ④ ore   ⑫ composite
       ⑤ ferrous   ⑬ pressure
       ⑥ furnace   ⑭ different
       ⑦ copper   ⑮ synthetics
       ⑧ carbon

(k) c wood, stone, lead, copper, iron, carbon, steel, ceramics, glass, porcelain, sintered-powder materials, composite materials, reinforced concrete, fibreglass

   d Schülerantworten

   e Gruppenarbeit

B2 Alloys

(k) a An alloy is a mixture of two or more metals.

(k) b Copper alloys (bronze and brass) are easier to cast and used for electrical systems. Steel (with carbon or carbon and silicon) is harder than iron and resistant to corrosion and is used for cars and ships, bridges, and buildings. Aluminium alloys are stronger than pure aluminium and used for aeroplanes, cars and household utensils. Pure gold, silver and titanium are too soft to work with, but their alloys are needed in dentistry, orthopaedic surgery, and for jewellery.

   c *

B3 Steel

- 1. alloy
  2. iron
  3. contain
  4. alloy steel
  5. amounts
  6. stainless
  7. containing
  8. producers
  9. electrical
  10. sheet steel

B4 Ceramics

a sinks, bathtubs, toilets, valves, ball bearings, spark plugs, tooth fillings/crowns, artificial hip joints, etc.

b elasticity, high electrical conductivity, softness

c Another example might be:
Ceramics are used in dentistry because of their chemical durability and their resistance against wear.

d Gruppenarbeit

B5 Plastics

a toys, kitchen and bathroom utensils, automobile and aerospace industries, garden furniture, packaging, casings for appliances (coffee machine, mixer, printer, razor/shaver)

b For products that should be heat resistant, thermosetting plastics should be used, because they harden permanently. These plastics have replaced dishes made of glass or porcelain to a large extent in the kitchen.
Packaging material is usually made of thermoplastics these days, which makes it recyclable.
Thermoplastic is a suitable material for e.g. picnic plates and cups, as long as they are properly recycled.

c ❶ engineering
❷ advantages
❸ raw
❹ coal
❺ granulate
❻ heat
❼ moulded

d Advantages: easily produced, necessary raw materials are abundant, simple processing, formable, recyclable, strength, wear resistance, light

Disadvantages: susceptible to heat and chemicals, cannot be disposed of by burning

e siehe Tapescript

(k) **f** polymethylmethacrylate = acrylics
polytetrafluoroethylene = Teflon
polyamide = nylon

(k) **g** acrylics: knitted sweaters, table-ware/dishes
nylon: women's stockings, clothing, hair- or toothbrush bristles, combs
Teflon: cookware, gaskets (Dichtungen), bearings (Lager)

B6 Mechanical properties of materials

(k) **a** Elasticity   The capability of a material to return to its original shape and size after being deformed.
Hardness   The resistance of materials to abrasion, cutting, etc. which is required for the moving parts of machines
Durability   The resistance of materials to corrosion, e.g. gold and platinum.
Ductility   This property allows materials to be stretched without losing their strength. …
Malleability The property of materials that can be worked into a new shape by hammering, rolling or pressing.

(k) **b** malleability malleable
hardness   hard
durability   durable

(k) **c** brittle   brittleness
conductive   conductivity
elastic   elasticity

(k) **d**
- Like ceramics, glass is very brittle, but it is not as durable.
- Copper is not elastic, but it is ductile. It has good electrical conductivity.
- Iron is hard, but it is brittle.
- The most important property of stainless steel is its durability. It is also malleable and elastic to a certain extent.
- Aluminium is malleable as well as ductile. It is also quite durable.

(i) **e** *Hier müssen nicht alle Beispiele gelöst werden, man kann sich auf cutting edges, antennas, springs und ball bearings beschränken.*

Lösungsbeispiele:

(k)
- Cutting edges must be made of extremely hard materials.
- Materials used for antennas must be elastic and durable.
- Screwdriver tips must be made of hardened metals.
- Valves have to be of hard material to withstand wear and heat.
- Ball bearings should last long. Therefore, they should be made of hard and durable material.

- Springs must be elastic and therefore are usually made of a special kind of high carbon steel.
- Door locks need the hardest possible and durable material.
- Materials used to build aeroplanes have to be light, elastic (especially for the wings) and durable.

B7 Elements and their physical properties

a carbon: >3550°C
   cobalt: 1495°C
   tungsten: 3380°C

b carbon: 6422°F
   cobalt: 2683°F
   tungsten: 6116°F

C Measurement and quality control
C1 Measuring tools

Für diesen Unitteil können die Schüler/innen Messmittel, die sie in ihrem Beruf verwenden, mitbringen, erklären und Messübungen durchführen. Für Klassen, die in ihrem Beruf keinen Messschieber verwenden, brauchen die Übungen c, d und e nicht durchgeführt zu werden. Wichtig: Zahlen und Dezimalzahlen vorher kurz wiederholen.

a 1. c
   2. b
   3. f
   4. g
   5. d
   6. e
   7. a

b 1. b
   2. g
   3. c
   4. d

c 1. a
   2. b
   3. d
   4. c
   5. h
   6. g
   7. e
   8. f

e 1. 32.3 mm
   2. 10.9 mm

C2 Units of measurement

- ❶ length
- ❷ amperes
- ❸ the base unit of light intensity
- ❹ kilograms
- ❺ kelvin
- ❻ temperature
- ❼ time
- ❽ moles

C3 ISO standards

(k) a Die ISO ist eine internationale Organisation für Standardisierung in Genf, gegründet 1947. Sie hat eine Reihe von international anerkannten Qualitätsstandards entwickelt für Produkte und Dienstleistungen. Firmen, die ein Qualitätssiegel nach ISO 9000 führen wollen, müssen sich einem Audit unterziehen und werden dann registriert.
Im Jahr 2000 wurden die Standards überarbeitet und an neuen Richtlinien orientiert:
ISO 9000 Konzepte und Terminologie
ISO 9001 Voraussetzungen für Qualitätssicherung
ISO 9004 Richtlinien für Qualitätsmanagement von Organisationen
ISO 19011 Richtlinien für Audits von Qualitätsmanagementsystemen

(k) b The ISO 9000 registration is proof to the customer that a company supplies assured quality products or services.

(k) c Beispiele: einheitliches Format von Telefon- und Kreditkarten (format of telephone and banking cards), einheitliche Maße von Frachtcontainern (dimensions of freight containers), SI-System (SI measurement system), Papiergrößen (paper sizes), einheitliche Symbole auf Automobilarmaturen (symbols for automobile controls), einheitlich genormte metrische Schraubengewinde (ISO metric screw threads)

d *Lösungsvorschlag:*
(k) International standardisation is needed, for example, in production to make sure that parts made in two different countries will all have the standard measurements and can be assembled in a third country.
The sizes of freight containers are standardised so that they can be transported on any truck to any port and loaded onto any ship.
Standardised credit cards can be used in shops and automatic tellers all around the world.

C4 Total Quality Management (TQM)

(k) a 1. Service industries and large manufacturing companies such as automobile producers, as well as small-to-medium enterprises, have installed quality management systems.
2. The quality, price and service of a product must be in line with the needs of the customers, and this is ensured by continuous improvement, for which all employees are responsible.
3. You can learn about quality control in special courses offered by technical colleges and private institutions.

(k) b 1, 3, 5

D Grammar revision: Gerund

a 1. presenting   4. seeing
    2. keeping   5. helping, developing
    3. taking   6. losing

b 1. calling   4. talking
    2. filling in   5. typing, to listen
    3. giving   6. loving

Unit 8
Energy and the environment

(i) Im Mittelpunkt dieser Unit stehen Fragen der Energieversorgung im 21. Jahrhundert mit ihren Auswirkungen auf die Umwelt. Im *Starter* kann am Beispiel des Weltenergieverbrauchs die Interpretation von Grafiken und Diagrammen eingeübt werden.

Im *A-Teil* werden die Ursachen und Auswirkungen des Treibhauseffekts dargestellt. Im *B-Teil* erfolgt eine Einführung in die wichtigsten erneuerbaren Energiearten, von Solarenergie über die Wasserkraft zur Windenergie. Der *C-Teil* der Unit beschäftigt sich mit dem Thema Kernenergie, vom traditionellen Kernkraftwerk zum Fusionsreaktor.

Abschließend sollen die Schüler/innen in einem SOL-Projekt Energieformen der Zukunft mit Hilfe des Internets recherchieren und vor den Mitschülern präsentieren. Dazu werden auf Seite 128 (im Schülerbuch) wichtige Tipps zur Präsentation gegeben.

Starter

(k) **a** The total world energy consumption has risen sharply within the past 30 years. It has almost doubled since 1971. Another considerable increase is predicted within the near future.

(k) **b** Oil is and will remain the most important single source of energy. In 1971 more than 2,000 million tons were consumed worldwide. This figure has risen dramatically since then: In the year 2000 we used up more than 30,000 million tons.

(k) **c** The most dramatic changes can be seen in the field of gas. Gas consumption more than doubled between the years 1971 and 1992. Since then there has been only a slight change with regard to that source of energy.

(k) **d** Almost no difference can be seen in the field of nuclear power. After a slight increase in the 1970s and 1980s there is no major change as far as nuclear power is concerned.

(k) **e** The category 'others' includes the so-called renewable sources of energy: mostly solar and wind power. Although these are becoming more important these days, the bar chart clearly shows that they are still only minor sources of energy.

A Global warming and the greenhouse effect

a "Global warming" describes an obvious tendency these days: the increase in the average world temperature. Science has chosen the term "greenhouse effect", as this rise in temperature can be compared to the rise in temperature in any greenhouse. The glass in a greenhouse and the gases in the atmosphere trap the heat in a similar way.

b 1. Without the greenhouse effect on earth the average temperature would be around 0° Celsius.

2. Carbon dioxide, CFC gases, methane and nitrous gases are responsible for this effect.

3. Carbon dioxide is caused by coal fires, volcanic eruptions, forest fires and mainly by the burning of oil. Coolants and aerosols often contain CFC gases. Cattle and fertilizers produce methane and nitrous gases.

4. The short-wave radiation of the sun penetrates the atmosphere, whereas the outgoing long-wave radiation is blocked by the atmospheric gases.

5. Most of the carbon dioxide and all the CFC gases as well as the methane and nitrous gases are produced by man.

6. Nature causes a smaller amount of carbon dioxide, e.g. in volcanic eruptions or in forest fires.

7. The effects of global warming can be enormous. The weather patterns could change. With the increase in temperature tropical diseases could spread into regions where they have been unknown so far.
With the melting of glaciers and the polar icecaps the sea levels could rise. All in all, the pollution levels on earth would rise.

c 1. average
2. surface
3. greenhouse effect
4. short-wave, long-wave
5. average
6. more violent, tropical, icecaps/glaciers, pollution

d 1. increase
2. emissions
3. is called
4. returned
5. effects

e 1. People can improve the technology of car engines to reduce the emissions of carbon dioxide.

2. We could reduce the emissions of our heating systems by installing improved burners.

3. CFC gases could be reduced by completely banning CFC-containing coolants and aerosols.

4. We could reduce the amount of fertilizers used in agriculture.

5. In coal power stations scrubbers have to be installed to reduce the amount of carbon dioxide.

A 1 Change of temperatures

(k) **a** It is evident that there has been a steady increase in the mean temperature in the course of the past 100 years.

(k) **b** It is quite obvious that the carbon dioxide concentration rose from 290 ppm in 1900 to 360 ppm in the year 2000.

(k) **c** There is clear evidence for the fact that with the increase of carbon dioxide the average world temperature is increasing as well. There has been a considerable increase in the carbon dioxide concentration within the past 100 years. In my opinion, this increase is responsible for the rising average temperature.

(k) **d** It is evident that there is a relationship between the increase of carbon dioxide and the rise of the average temperature on earth. The reasons for this trend are quite obvious.

On the one hand, the combustion engines of cars must be seen as main polluters. With a steady increase in the number of cars all over the world there is bound to be an increase in carbon dioxide. From my point of view, scientists have to improve the technology of motor car engines as soon as possible. First of all, the fuel-cell technology offers a promising solution to this problem. In my opinion, we have to give up the traditional combustion engine within the next 10 years and introduce the electric car driven by fuel cells. This would be the best way to reduce the carbon dioxide concentration in the earth's atmosphere.

On the other hand, heating systems in private households have to be modernised as well. A high amount of carbon dioxide is produced by outdated heaters.

In addition, we have to consider new types of public transportation, which should be cheap and attractive to convince more commuters to leave their cars in the garage.

There are other factors which contribute to an increase of carbon dioxide: Coal power stations, for example, are often outdated. Chemical filters – so-called scrubbers – have to be installed everywhere. In my opinion this would help a lot.

Summing up all the arguments, I am convinced that we have a chance to get rid of this problem only by taking a whole series of actions now.

A 2 Rise in sea levels

a 1. The global mean temperature could rise by about 4°C within 50 years.

2. The effects on the world's climate and weather patterns would be enormous. While the tropical areas are expected to get a little warmer, the colder regions on earth would get a lot warmer. The weather would become unpredictable – droughts might occur in areas where they are unknown so far; other areas would experience a lot more storms.

3. In the past, changes of temperature took place over very long periods (sometimes 10,000 years) – nature was therefore able to adapt. This time nature and mankind have only got 50 years to get used to these new circumstances.

4. An increase of only 0.5°C would already cause a rise in sea levels of about 10–15 cm. This could lead to flooding in coastal areas.

5. Pessimistic calculations say that we will see a 2-m rise in sea levels within half a century!

6. Agriculture would be most negatively affected. Although we do not know exactly what is going to happen where, we are quite sure that in some areas agriculture will no longer be possible.

7. This could become a reality if the Gulf Stream changed its direction away from Europe (maybe towards Canada?).

b 1. mean
2. rise, predicted
3. alter
4. adjust
5. think
6. droughts
7. disastrously
8. shifts

c 1. difference
2. climate
3. dramatically
4. pessimistic
5. predict
6. prepare
7. frequent
8. disastrously

B Renewable sources of energy

a ❶ renewable
❷ derived
❸ depleted
❹ converted
❺ combustion
❻ efficiency

Unit 8

b

Source of energy	Pros	Cons
Solar power	– Does not cause any pollution – Can be turned directly into electricity – Heat of the sun can be used to heat up water for household use – Sunlight can be focused via mirrors to run a conventional steam turbine	– Most effective in summer when less energy is needed – Efficiency is relatively low – Solar panels are still too expensive – Huge areas have to be covered by solar panels or mirrors to generate enough energy
Wind power	– Does not produce harmful emissions – Most effective when the wind blows (in winter) – Very efficient in coastal regions	– Wind generators are noisy – Some people say the windmills/turbines deface the landscape (also a kind of pollution) – Too many generators are necessary to produce enough energy
Tidal power	– The flow of the tides offers an excellent chance to generate electricity – Absolutely predictable source of energy (permanent flow of tides) – Free of pollution	– Possible only in coastal regions – Might negatively affect nature (huge dams have to be built) – Wildlife might be endangered

(k) c Nuclear power is produced by burning a rare kind of uranium. The basic material is found underground in rocks. Therefore, it has to be mined and chemically treated before it can be used in a power plant. All in all, it is a limited source of energy, like coal and oil.

B 1 Solar power

(k) a We can apply two principal technologies to produce energy from sunlight. With the help of solar cells we can generate electricity in a direct way. By using solar panels we are able to heat up water for domestic households, for example.

(k) b Solar cells are semiconductor devices; i.e. two different types of silicon layers are connected by a wire, thus producing an electric current. Each solar cell generates a small amount of electricity of about 0.5 volts. By connecting the solar cells in series, a higher amount of electricity can be generated.

(k) c With the help of solar panel technology we can heat water to such a high temperature that it turns into steam. This steam can be used to run a steam turbine, which then generates electricity in a traditional way.

d 1. solar panels   5. inverters
     2. warranty   6. kit
     3. applications   7. gadget
     4. state-of-the-art   8. battery charger

e

Deutsche Sonnenkollektoren GmbH   *Allee 65*
                                                      70469 Stuttgart

Our ref.: DS 23/1

SOLAR Products Ltd.
11-13 Sha Tsui Road
Hong Kong

Dear Sir or Madam,

We have read the advertisement about your company in the Internet. As we are very interested in your range of solar power products, we would like to have some details about what you offer. Please send us additional information about the costs of your solar cells and solar panels. In addition, we are interested in the efficiency of your products. Furthermore, we would like to be informed about your terms of delivery and payment. We would appreciate it if you could send us some of your brochures including price lists. Please include details about possible discounts for large orders.

We look forward to hearing from you.

Yours faithfully,

Peter Mayer

Peter Mayer
Managing Director

B 2 Water power

a Electricity can be generated with the help of water in hydroelectric power stations. In addition, the power of the tides can be harnessed to generate electricity, and last but not least even the kinetic energy of waves can be used to generate electricity.

(k) **b** For a pumped storage system two reservoirs are built at different levels. As the water rushes down from the higher to the lower reservoir the kinetic energy of the water can be used to turn a turbine. In this way electricity can be generated during peak hours. At night, when energy consumption is low, the water is pumped back up to the higher reservoir for the peak hour of the next day. Environmentalists dislike this technology because a lot of energy is needed to pump up the water at night – energy which has to be produced by other types of power stations such as nuclear power plants.

(k) **c** The production of electricity from tidal power has one big disadvantage. Low and high tides occur at regular intervals but not necessarily when there is a high demand for energy. Production may be high at night when energy consumption is low.
In tidal power stations energy is generated by turbines in a more or less traditional way. The turbine turns with the flow of water and produces electricity with the help of electromagnetism.

(k) **d** Although there is a permanent movement of the sea which can be harnessed to generate electricity, the disadvantage of wave power is the very low efficiency of an individual float. Therefore, huge areas of the sea have to be covered with floats in order to generate enough electricity.

(k) **e** 1. different
2. generate
3. moreover
4. need
5. demand
6. stored
7. almost
8. reliable
9. disadvantage
10. motion

B 3 Wind power

(k) **a** Wind has always been a source of energy. In former times wind was the only source for ships sailing the world. In addition, windmills were used in agriculture for grinding corn or pumping water.

(k) **b** Aerogenerators can be used only in areas with a high frequency of strong winds. The most reliable areas are along coastlines and on top of mountain ranges.

(k) **c** As wind is never completely predictable, we cannot rely on it as our sole source of energy.

(k) **d** – You can use wood as a building material. But the hotels should be relatively small so that not too much wood is used up.
– I would prefer the southeast coast for building the small hotels. The sunny, hot climate allows solar technology to be used as a source of energy. The

tourists wouldn't like the windy western part of the island anyhow, as swimming could be too dangerous.
- Solar energy as a main source is advisable, and wind power could be harnessed from the westen part of the island.
- The forests could be destroyed by the building activities. The government must make sure that when trees are chopped down for building, new trees are planted right away.
- The local way of life would be changed; the people may benefit financially but they may have to deal with noise pollution and crowding. The water supply must be kept clean and demand must not exceed supply.

e *Diese Übung eignet sich dazu, in Gruppen Informationen zu einzelnen erneuerbaren Energieformen im Internet zu sammeln und in Form einer Präsentation (eventuell mit Hilfe von Computerprogrammen) vorzustellen. Zur Bearbeitung und zum Erstellen der Präsentation sollte den Gruppen genügend Zeit eingeräumt werden. Der Lehrer/die Lehrerin sollte darauf achten, dass das ganze Spektrum erneuerbarer Energien behandelt wird.*

C Nuclear fission and nuclear fusion (C1/C2)

a 1. The most powerful fusion accelerator is in Albuquerque.
2. To start a reaction a 100-trillion-watt pulse of electricity is necessary.
3. A pea-sized pellet is directed towards the pulse of deuterium gas.
4. The plasma is heated to millions of degrees for a few billionths of a second.
5. All efforts to produce a controlled nuclear fusion have not succeeded so far.

b The worst problem is the high temperature which is necessary to start a reaction. So far we have not been able to reach this temperature long enough to achieve a fusion of nuclei. Another problem is the high temperatures involved in the process when fusion takes place. No material on earth can resist such a temperature.

c Nuclear fission involves too many unsolved problems. Apart from the danger of accidents at nuclear power stations, there is the problem of nuclear waste which has to be stored in an absolutely safe way for thousands and thousands of years. Even if we solved the problem of nuclear waste, an accident like Chernobyl could happen again. Whole regions would no longer be habitable. Furthermore, there is the possibility of terrorist attacks on nuclear power stations.

Unit 8

C 3 Project work.
Internet search: Future sources of energy

(i) *In einer gemeinsamen brain-storming session (eventuell mit Metaplan-Technik) betrachten die Schüler/innen mögliche Energieformen der Zukunft und schreiben diese an die Tafel.*

Die Gruppen wählen sich je eine Energieform aus, um diese mit Hilfe des Internets im Detail zu durchleuchten. Dabei eignen sich für die Recherche im Internet zum Einstieg in die Thematik am ehesten die Metasuchmaschinen. Die dabei erarbeiteten Ergebnisse müssen für die Präsentation komprimiert und aufbereitet werden. Die Übersicht auf Seite 128 (Schülerbuch) soll dabei für die Präsentation als Grundlage dienen.

Die Präsentation der Schüler/innen kann – insbesondere bei leistungsstarken Klassen und falls die technischen Voraussetzungen dazu vorliegen – mit Hilfe von Präsentationsprogrammen am Computer vorbereitet und danach mit Beamer vor der Klasse präsentiert werden. Diese Übung eignet sich besonders für selbstorganisierte Lernformen. So können im Internet neben Informationen zu neuen Technologien auch Bilder bzw. Filmsequenzen herunter geladen werden. Aber auch andere Formen der Präsentation wie beispielsweise Folien sind durchaus denkbar, insbesondere wenn die technischen Voraussetzungen nicht vorhanden sind.

D Grammar revision: Participle (present and past)

(k) **a** 1. guaranteeing
2. being
3. being built
4. converted
5. improving
6. planning
7. renovating

(k) **b** 1. Example
2. Scientists have studied the greenhouse effect, attributing it to the rise in emissions from industry and cars.
3. After having gathered information from the Internet, they started work on their presentation.
4. Before ordering the battery charger, the secretary asked for a price list.
5. Not having achieved a major breakthrough in fusion, we must continue with research in renewable sources of energy.
6. Scientists working in nuclear power stations are often supporters of this technology.
7. The wind farms built along the coast generate enough energy for 5,000 households.
8. Water stored behind a dam possesses potential energy.
9. Knowing that pollution is not only caused by cars, we should take steps to reduce the emissions.
10. When describing renewable energies, you must not forget water power.

c 1. Before starting to install the solar panel, the owner of the house studied the instructions.
2. Having become very popular, solar energy has developed into a very environmentally friendly source of energy.
3. Not being able to understand English, he could not read the instructions for the solar panel.
4. We ordered the solar panel after having read the advertisement.
5. While reading the ad, he was listening to some music.

Unit 9 Business trips

ⓘ Im *Unitteil A* geht es um die Planung einer Reise nach Philadelphia. Eine deutsche Firma, die Folientastaturen herstellt (Folientastaturen sind Tastaturen mit einigen wenigen Tasten bis hin zu einer kompletten PC-Tastatur, die unter einer wasser- und schmutzabweisenden Folie geschützt sind) möchte eine Zweigstelle an der amerikanischen Ostküste gründen. Nachdem Grundstücksfragen bereits geklärt sind, braucht die Firma natürlich dringend Arbeitskräfte und die möchte man auf der Tech Expo USA, einer (tatsächlich existierenden Arbeitsplatzbörse) gewinnen.
Zwei britische Mitarbeiter planen die Reise. Hier geht es um Flugpläne und die Buchung eines geeigneten Fluges, um die Suche nach dem geeigneten Hotel, um das Verfassen von Memo und Fax und um das Telefonieren mit der Rezeption eines Hotels .
Teil B behandelt die Ankunft in Philadelphia, Einchecken im Hotel und das Mieten eines Autos.
Der *Teil C* befasst sich mit den kulturellen Aspekten einer solchen Geschäftsreise. Dazu gehören die historischen Sehenswürdigkeiten Philadelphias und auch der Restaurantbesuch inklusive einer ausführlichen Speisekarte.
Teil D – Grammar Revision – behandelt die if-clauses.

ⓘ Philadelphia wird in den letzten Jahren als der Standort für Zukunftstechnologien gehandelt. Einige deutsche Firmen haben dort bereits Niederlassungen mit über 1000 Mitarbeitern gegründet. Philadelphia ist als Wirtschaftsstandort gut geeignet. Es liegt verkehrsgünstig zwischen Washington und New York, hat einen gut ausgebauten Hafen und eine gute Straßenanbindung. Der Flughafen wird national und international gut bedient und auch erschlossenes Gelände auf früheren Industriebrachen ist z.Zt. noch günstig zu erhalten. Außerdem gibt es für Hochtechnologien ein sehr gutes Arbeitskräftepotential durch Abgänger der örtlichen Universitäten wie Drexel University, Temple University und The University of Pennsylvania, an der übrigens der erste Computer ENIAC entwickelt worden war. Zudem stimmt das kulturelle Umfeld. Philadelphia ist die Wiege der amerikanischen Nation (es war Ende des 19. Jahrhunderts für zehn Jahre Hauptstadt), das historische Zentrum ist sehenswert, die Küche international und auf hohem Niveau; Konzerte, Kunstausstellungen, Museen und Theater schaffen ein lebenswertes Ambiente. Schulen und Universitäten in Philadelphia und Umgebung genießen hohes Ansehen. Erfreulich für deutsche Firmen kommt noch hinzu, dass die Stadt viele deutschstämmige Einwohner hat (mit zwei großen Einwanderungswellen nach 1840 und nach dem 2. Weltkrieg), die Menschen dort also deutschen Firmen offener gegenüber stehen als vielleicht in manchen anderen amerikanischen Städten.

ⓘ **Orthographie:** *Es ist sinnvoll, zu Beginn der Unit auf die unterschiedliche Orthographie zwischen dem britischen und amerikanischen Englisch einzugehen (siehe auch Seite 112). Die Lektionstexte sind wie das ganze Buch im britischen Englisch gehalten, bei Originaltexten z.B. aus dem Internet werden die Schüler/innen aber auf die orthographischen Unterschiede stoßen.*

Starter

a 1. The Customs Declaration form is filled out on the airplane prior to landing in the USA and is handed over with collected baggage before the passenger may leave the airport.

    2. The yellow folder is a car rental contract containing the conditions of rental and payment and service telephone numbers for use while under way.

    3. There is a map of the USA, probably of the roads in one region.

    4. The green and white card is part of the airline ticket issued for the route from Frankfurt to Philadelphia.

    5. The dark-red booklet is a passport issued by the United Kingdom. It is the main identification of citizenship and must be shown for entry to a foreign country and for re-entry into the United Kingdom.

    6. The three gray-green notes are a 5-, a 10-, and a 100-dollar bill from the United States of America.

b – Plan the itinerary, where you will be and when.
    – Make reservations for the necessary flights.
    – Reserve a hotel/hotels.
    – Arrange for a rental car to be waiting at the airport where you will arrive.
    – Make sure that your travel documents are valid, i.e. passport, visa if required, international driver's licence.
    – Obtain a guidebook about the area you will be visiting and/or a small phrase book to help with the language spoken there.
    – Exchange some money, if a different currency than the Euro is used where you are going, so that you will have at least enough to cover small expenses on your first day there.

A A business trip / A1 Planning a trip

a The advertisement promotes the Philadelphia area as a place for industry to settle or expand, given that it has become a centre of information technology.

b Philacon Valley is a take off on the name Silicon Valley, given to the area in California where the computer industry settled and boomed during the 1980s. @Philly makes use of the familiar symbol for an e-mail address and the colloquial nickname for Philadelphia. Technophilly does the same by referring to technology as a dominant industry in the Philadelphia area.

c ❶ wants   ❻ will be finished
    ❷ have decided   ❼ have arranged
    ❸ agreed   ❽ hope
    ❹ have…been finalized   ❾ were chosen
    ❺ have been bought

(k) **d** Philadelphia in August; hotels, flights, car rental; arrive 2–3 days early; direct flight, no stopover; hotel near city centre; international driver's licence; cultural, historic area, restaurants

(k) **e** 1. wrong 4. wrong
2. wrong 5. not given
3. is given 6. wrong

(k) **f** First they need to call a travel agency to book a suitable flight. Then they have to arrange for a hotel in Philadelphia. They must check that their passports are still valid, and they should arrange for a rental car and apply for international driver's licences. They have to search for cultural events in the Internet so that they will know where to take their customers. They shouldn't forget to pick up their plane tickets, but they needn't take a taxi to the airport because a friend can drive them.

A2 Making hotel reservations

(k) **a** The All-Seasons Hotel appears to be better for Valerie and Chris because it offers more of the things they requested. The advertisement for the Denton Inn does not mention a newsstand, no-smoking rooms, or non-allergenic pillows. The All-Seasons offers a fitness room as well as exercise equipment in the room. It also offers valet parking, which is only for an extra charge at the Denton Inn, and since they will be staying for several days and want to rent a car, they will be using this service. The All-Seasons also has check-in at any time, whereas the official time by which guests should check in at the Denton Inn is stated as 3 p.m. and as Valerie and Chris are flying from Europe they will probably not arrive until late afternoon or early evening. Audio-visual equipment is offered for a charge at the Denton Inn, but free of charge at the All-Seasons, and they may want to make a presentation to their customers. Finally, since they do want to take advantage of what the city offers culturally, it makes more sense to stay in the city centre, given that the All-Seasons offers an airport shuttle service.

(k) **b** Sample sentences: The hotel should have a shuttle service to the airport. It should be close to the centre of the city but in a quiet area. An exercise room should be available, and the room should have a bathroom with a shower. It would be very convenient to have a refrigerator, a coffee maker and a hairdryer in the room. There must be a telephone and a dataport in the room. Ideal for me would be a hotel with a conference room, and it would be fun to have a pool.

c Gruppenarbeit

d

KeySys Membrane Switches and Keyboards
1215 Grüneberg Straße
Frankfurt, Germany
Tel. ...

Fax Message

The All-Seasons Hotel
Logan Square
Philadelphia, PA

Dear Sir or Madam

We would like to book two quiet single rooms with shower for six nights, from August 25 (day of arrival) until August 31 (day of departure). They are for our employees Ms V. Piskei and Mr C. Fehily, who are both nonsmokers. Please quote the daily rate and advise whether breakfast is included in the price.
They would like to be picked up at Philadelphia International Airport. We will fax you the time of their arrival.
Please confirm our booking as soon as possible, and let us know which credit cards you accept.

Yours faithfully

Claudia Schneider,
Secretary

e
– Keine Zimmer zur Verfügung im All-Seasons Hotel.
– Zimmer gebucht im Royal Excelsior Hotel, näher am Flughafen.
– Buchung muss schnellstens bestätigt werden.

f Schülerantworten
N.B. Fasching = Mardi Gras in New Orleans or Carnival in Rio de Janeiro,
Pfingsten = Whitsuntide or Pentecost,
Christi Himmelfahrt = Ascension Day,
Fronleichnam = Corpus Christi Day,
Buß- und Bettag = nothing comparable in the United States

Example: Erntedank is celebrated in the United States as Thanksgiving but in November, not in October as in Germany.

g Schülerantworten

(k)

h Receptionist	Chris
Royal Excelsior Hotel, Mike Turner speaking. Can I help you?	Yes, my name is Chris Fehily, I am calling from Germany. We had some problems with a reservation …
Oh I am sorry to hear that, when did you book for?	No, I am sorry we didn't book at your hotel, we wanted to book at the All-Seasons Hotel for August 25.
I am sorry, but this is the Hampton Inn, would you like me to give you the number of the Four Seasons Hotel?	There seems to be a misunderstanding; let me explain. We requested two single rooms at the All-Seasons Hotel. This morning they sent me a fax telling me that they are booked up due to the national holiday. They said they had made arrangements with you for August 25 to August 31, and they told me I should call you right away.
Oh, now I understand. I really have to apologise. I'll check with the booking department right away. Who did you say made the arrangement?	On my fax here it says Carlos Montinez.
Yes, I've got that. Please hold the line, I'll be right back. … Yes, we had a call from the All-Seasons Hotel. The dates are the 25th as the day of arrival and the 31st of August as the day of departure. Two single rooms.	Are they single rooms with shower?
I am afraid not, one is with bath.	That's okay. – And can you pick us up from the airport?
No problem, sir; there is always a limousine parked at the west exit, and if there shouldn't be one use our phone right next to the booth.	Well I am certainly glad we have that settled! Thank you very much.
You're welcome, sir. And if you should have any more questions concerning your stay or the services of our hotel make sure to call us right away.	We'll do that. Thank you and goodbye.
Bye and have a nice trip, sir.	

A3 Booking a flight

a, b DL 107 ca. 11:35, US 893 ca. 15:15, EA 555 ca. 17:20; therefore, they should choose US flight 893.   (k)

c Gruppenarbeit   (k)

d
Customer:	I want to fly to Boston on July 15, but I don't want to leave too early in the day.
Agent:	I'm afraid the only seat we have available is on an early morning flight departing at 7:30 a.m.
Customer:	I'd prefer a non-stop flight.
Agent:	Sorry, this one does have a 30-minute stopover in New York.
Customer:	I'd like to have a window seat in one of the front rows, but I don't suppose that's possible. And I don't want to be near the smoking area.
Agent:	No, there are no window seats free, just an aisle seat in row 32, which is near the back of the plane. However, no smoking is allowed on any of our flights.
Customer:	I'll be carrying only hand luggage. Can I go through express check-in to avoid waiting/standing in line?
Agent:	I'm very sorry, but there is no express check-in service for international flights, due to the increased need for security. However, if you plan your next trip earlier, there will be more flights to choose from and you'll surely be able to have a window seat.

(k)

e Partnerarbeit

Additional text with exercises: Checking in at the airport   Zusatz

Before Valerie and Chris can check in and get rid of their luggage, they have to answer the following questions put by the security guard of EuroAmerican Airlines.

1. Who packed your luggage?
2. Where have you left your luggage between the time you packed it and now?
3. Have you ever left your luggage unattended?
4. Has anyone given you anything to carry with you on this flight?
5. Are you carrying any electronic items with you, such as a hairdryer, a movie camera, a razor, a cell phone, a CD player, or a computer?
6. Has any electronic item of yours been repaired lately?
7. Are you carrying any weapons or sharp items with you?

Zusatz

a Discuss the reasons for these questions.

b Match the questions with the following answers (number with letter):

a. I haven't taken anything from anyone.
b. As I said, I never left it unattended.
c. No repairs whatsoever.
d. I packed it myself.
e. All I can think of is a little pocket knife.
f. I always had my luggage with me.
g. I have a hairdryer and a small camera; my cell phone is switched off, and I have a palm-top to work with on the plane.

(k) Key: 1.d 2.f 3.b 4.a 5.g 6.c 7.e

(i) **Additional information about Philadelphia International Airport.**

Philadelphia International Airport is one of the most convenient airports on the American East Coast. It still has less air traffic than, for example, John F. Kennedy Airport in New York or Logan Airport in Boston. The terminals in Philadelphia are spacious, the immigration officers are as friendly as you would expect them to be in the "city of brotherly love", as it is called due to its Quaker origins; no one rushes the arriving guests with loud voices into the correct lanes for passport control. Not only are they friendly, they even have boxes with tissues beneath their desks in case somebody sneezes while their passport is being checked!

B Arriving in Philadelphia
B1 At the Airport

(k) **a**
KARIN	= 2	50 E. Broadway	= 8
06.05.72	= 3	KRÜGER	= 1
LH 2479	= 6	GERMANY	= 4
3346899920 B	= 5	FRANKFURT	= 7

Achtung: Das Datum *06.05.72* wird in Amerika als *June 5, 1972* gelesen!

(k) **b** is on time = wird pünktlich ankommen
has been cancelled = ist annulliert
is delayed by 30 min = hat 30 Minuten Verspätung
has landed = ist angekommen/gelandet
now departing = fährt/fliegt jetzt ab

c 1. no (unless your name is Mr. Fernandez)
   2. no (unless you are planning on taking a further flight to a city within the United States)
   3. no
   4. yes
   5. no (unless your name is Mary Watson)
   6. no

B2 Checking in at the hotel

a 1 = reservation   4 = breakfast   7 = gym   10 = stay
   2 = shower   5 = available   8 = rent
   3 = floor   6 = call   9 = major

B3 At the car rental desk

a Since there are only the two of them, a compact at the special weekend rate would be the most favourable arrangement. They will have no problem with the stipulation that they return the car to the original rental office, and as Chris is an early riser, he can return it by the 8:00 a.m. deadline.

b A full-size type-C car would probably be best, since it would offer more room for the baggage. It can also be returned to the airport instead of to the original rental office, even though this means a charge of $25 more.

c The mid-size B-type car would be the best, as there are no restrictions on when it must be returned.

C Cultural aspects

Zusatzinformation für den Lehrer / die Lehrerin:

An old memory rhyme lists the four streets from the center of the city north and south and ends in a riddle:
   Market, Arch, Race and Vine,
   Chestnut, Walnut, Spruce and Pine.
   Can you spell all that in seven letters?
   (a-l-l-t-h-a-t)
Note that Chestnut Street is between Walnut and Market, but the name cannot be seen on the part of the map shown in the book, p. 141.

a The City Tavern is on 2nd Street north of Walnut Street.
   Betsy Ross House is located on Arch Street just east of 3rd Street.
   Independence Hall is on Chestnut Street between 5th and 6th Streets.

Unit 9

(k) **b** We could begin at the Independence Seaport Museum at Penn's Landing and then walk west on Walnut Street to 2nd, turning north to stop at the City Tavern. After pausing there for something to drink, we could walk west on Chestnut Street to Independence Hall to see where the Declaration of Independence was signed. Right nearby is Carpenter's Hall, with an exhibition of old tools. One block north is the famous Liberty Bell.

(i)
> **Info: A pretzel vendor**
> On their walk through the city Valerie and Chris see something that looks very much like a hot dog stand. But it isn't. The street vendor is selling something that they certainly would not have expected to see in the USA – pretzels, very much like those that you can get in the southern part of Germany. These pretzels date back to the many German immigrants who came to the city beginning around 1830. They are soft, sprinkled with salt, and are eaten with yellow mustard. For visitors from Germany, of course, it's OK to eat them without mustard.

C2 Eating out

a Schülerantworten

(k) **b** Beef/Veal: Roast Prime Rib of Beef
Pork: none
Lamb: Rack of Lamb
Poultry: Roasted Duckling, Chicken Breast Madeira,
       Thai Green Chicken Curry
Game: Medallions of Venison
Fish: none as main course, but Smoked Pennsylvania Brook Trout
    as first course
Seafood: Tavern Lobster Pie
Vegetarian: Veggie Omelette

c

(k) Gemüse der Saison = seasonal vegetable(s)　　Spargel = asparagus
Spinat = spinach　　Gurke = cucumber
Fruchtlikör = cordials　　Rehfleisch = venison
Kräutertee = herb tea　　Blätterteig = filo pastry
Lammrücken = rack of lamb　　Junge Ente = duckling
Forelle = (brook) trout　　gefüllte Garnele = stuffed shrimp
Lachs = salmon

(k) **d** Smoked Pennsylvania Brook Trout, Roast Prime Rib of Beef, and Creme Caramel.

e Tavern Soup (depending on the contents) or Tavern Country Salad, Veggie Omelette, and Baklava or Creme Caramel. (k)

f 5, 3, 6, 2, 1, 4 (k)

g Could I have the menu, please? (k)
What can you recommend?
Is it very spicy/hot? Is it with meat?
I think I'll have the steak. I like it rare/medium/well-done.
Could I have some more salt/pepper/wine/water...?
Could I have the bill (or check), please? Can I pay by ... card?

D Grammar revision: If-clauses (Conditionals)

a 1. knew
2. would/could call
3. are
4. had contacted
5. wouldn't have started
6. turns out

b 1. Wenn wir in einen Stau geraten, werden wir unser Flug verpassen. (k)
2. Wir müssten uns jetzt keine Sorgen machen, wenn wir uns früher abgemeldet hätten.
3. Wann kämst du in Chicago an, wenn du den Flug mit Zwischenlandung in Pittsburgh nehmen würdest?
4. Was wirst du für deine Mutter kaufen, wenn du Zeit hast, um in den Zoll-Freien Laden einzukaufen?
5. Wo isst deine Freundin normalerweise, wenn sie in Chicago übernachten muss?
6. Wenn ihr ein Restaurant gefällt, besucht sie ihn gewöhnlich wieder.

c 1. If the project is successful we will have a reason to celebrate. (k)
2. If we had been better prepared we would surely have been finished sooner.
3. What kind of job would you like to have if you had the chance to work in America?
4. If I'm not in the office on a Friday evening I can usually be reached at my girlfriend's place.
6. If you can't reach me at all, please leave a message on my mailbox.

Unit 10
Finding a job in Europe

Die Unit 10 behandelt ausgehend von Europa die durch die Globalisierung ausgelösten Veränderungen in der heutigen Arbeitswelt. Im Starter sollen die Schüler/innen ihre Kenntnisse über die Mitgliedsstaaten und assoziierten Länder der EU reaktivieren.

Im *A-Teil* der Unit erhalten die Schüler/innen Einblick in die veränderte Arbeitswelt von heute. Am konkreten Beispiel der Aufenthalts- und Arbeitsbedingungen im Vereinigten Königreich (exemplarisch für alle Mitgliedsstaaten der EU) werden im *Teil B1* die heutigen Möglichkeiten bei der Arbeitsplatzsuche im europäischen Ausland vorgestellt. Die *Teile B2* und *B3* zeigen den immer wichtiger werdenden Bereich der Telearbeit auf. Der *Teil C* gibt ausgehend vom Themenbereich „Bewerbung" Hinweise zum Erstellen eines Lebenslaufs und zum Bewerbungsgespräch. Der *Teil C3* rundet mit dem Thema „Greencard" den Bereich Arbeitswelt ab.

Die *Grammatik* im *Teil D* behandelt die verschiedenen Formen der Zukunft im Englischen.

Starter

Country	International letter symbol	Nationality	Language(s)
Austria	A	Austrian	German
Belgium	B	Belgian	French + Flemish
Denmark	DK	Danish	Danish
Finland	FIN	Finnish	Finnish
France	F	French	French
Germany	D	German	German
Greece	GR	Greek	Greek
Ireland	IRL	Irish	English
Italy	I	Italian	Italian
Luxembourg	L	Luxembourger	French + German
The Netherlands	NL	Dutch	Dutch
Portugal	P	Portuguese	Portuguese
Spain	E	Spanish	Spanish
Sweden	S	Swedish	Swedish
United Kingdom	GB	British	English

A Our workplace is changing

a From my point of view, Claudette is right. Already today more and more communication is taking place via the Internet.
I would say that Marco is right as far as production is concerned. On the other hand, I am absolutely convinced that there will still be jobs for low-skilled workers in our country.
It is a fact that more people will have access to the Internet, but I don't agree with Nadja as far as the selling of goods via the Internet is concerned. People will still prefer to go to a shop. I would say that is an experience we wouldn't want to miss.

b From my point of view, foreign languages will be more important in our future economy. Most important will be English as the "lingua franca". Let me give you an example: Suppose I worked in Portugal – this would not necessarily mean that I have to speak Portuguese. I could well imagine doing my business there in English. Surely, the mobility of everybody will definitely increase. More and more people will work in foreign countries, but they will all stay in contact with their home country via the Internet. I could even imagine being employed as a teleworker for an international company. In order to be competitive we will have to go on learning for the rest of our lives. Nobody can sit back and relax. New technologies will have to be adopted continually.
We will truly live in a global village. There is one advantage for the consumer: because of global competition the quality of goods will continue to improve. I think everybody agrees when I say that individual nations will be less important. We must act and think globally. New ways of communication will help us to do so.

B Working in Europe
B 1 Working in the United Kingdom

b Working and living in Britain – no longer a problem

The "United States of Europe" is no longer a distant dream, as Europe is growing together. European Community law guarantees the same rights to all nationals of the European Union. It is much easier today to work and live in Britain than you might expect. If you live in the European Union and if you possess a passport of a member country it is up to you to decide where you want to live and work. In Britain, for example, you will be treated like any British national. You don't even have to register with the police. If your family wants to join you in Britain, they will have the same possibilities. You don't need a work permit – you can even start your own business there. The British authorities will even welcome the decision, because you might be a future taxpayer.

(k) c – European Economic Area (EEA) nationals: apart from the European Union there are the following member countries: Iceland, Liechtenstein and Norway.
– People born in Gibraltar.
– Commonwealth citizens who were allowed to enter or to remain in the UK on the basis that a grandparent was born there.
– Husbands, wives and dependent children under 18 of people who hold work permits.

Under the Immigration Rules a person does not need a work permit if he or she qualifies under one of the following categories and has obtained prior entry clearance at a British Diplomatic Post abroad:

– Those coming to the UK to set up a new business or to take over or join an existing business as a partner or director.
– Ministers of religion.
– Representatives of overseas newspapers, news agencies and broadcasting organisations.
– Representatives of overseas firms who are seeking to establish a UK branch or subsidiary.
– Employees of an overseas government coming to do a job for their government.

The list continues – one thing the people in the second group have in common is that they are specialists with individual rights.

(k) d – Iceland, Liechtenstein and Norway are member countries of the European Economic Area; although they are not officially members of the European Union they have exactly the same rights.
– Gibraltar is a crown colony of the United Kingdom. Therefore, its people have the same rights as persons living in the UK.
– The Commonwealth status guarantees these special rights – they were agreed upon when Britain joined the European Union in 1973.

B 2 Telework – Facts and figures

(k) a 1. Telework has become one of the main issues of the European Union. The Lisbon Summit decided to develop telework continually in order to achieve a real global information society.
2. They want Europe to become the most advanced knowledge-based economy in the world. This would create better jobs and an improved social cohesion in Europe.
3. Finland, with 17% of its work force employed in telework, has the highest percentage in Europe.
4. Spain, with only 2.8% of teleworkers, is at the bottom of the list.
5. The United Kingdom, with more than 500,000 home-based teleworkers, has the highest total number.
6. Germany, with more than 500,000 self-employed teleworkers.

b Possible additional answers:

Advantages for business	Advantages for the individual
in times of economic growth more people can be employed	teleworkers work in their home offices
in times of economic recession it is easier to reduce the number of employees	it is good for women who still have to raise children
the risk for the employer is relatively low	the amount of work is decided individually
freelance workers are employed for only a special task	it doesn't matter where you live, as the work is received and delivered via the Internet
flexibility for companies is enormous	you can live in Greece but work for a British company

c *Die Schüler/innen ordnen die unter b gefundenen Argumente nach sinnvollen Gesichtspunkten und präsentieren die Ergebnisse als Vortrag unter Anwendung moderner Präsentationstechniken.*

d – Teleworkers have only temporary contracts.
 – Planning for the future is very difficult, as you never know how long you will be employed.
 – Teleworkers have to develop their own pension schemes (high costs are involved).
 – Sickness benefits have to be planned on an individual basis (high costs).
 – As a teleworker you depend very much on a booming economy; in times of recession less work will be offered and that means less money as well.

B3 Are you ready for telework?

a–e Schülerantworten

Zur Beantwortung der Fragen müssen die Schüler/innen online arbeiten. Zum Einstieg eignet sich die Homepage von ETO. Die Daten werden regelmäßig aktualisiert. Die Recherche im Internet sollte in Kleingruppen durchgeführt werden. In Anschluss an diese Arbeit berichten die Schüler/innen mündlich über ihre Ergebnisse.

C Jobs, job application and interview
C1 Job application

(k) **a**
1. responsible
2. implementation
3. essential requirements
4. current
5. deadlines
6. completion
7. scheduling
8. negotiable
9. hands-on approach
10. preferably

b Schülerantworten

(k) **c**

Dear Mr White

I would like to apply for the job of Technical Consultant advertised in Science and Technology. Since completing my education I have been working for Wittmann GmbH, a car component supplier, where I am Technical Assistant to the Sales Director. My duties include quality control and budget planning.

I feel that my technical knowledge and in particular my language abilities in English, French and Spanish are ideally suited to a position in an internationally operating company.

Thank you for considering my application. If you need any further information, please write or call me.

Yours sincerely

Carsten Berger

d Individuelle Schülerlösungen in Anlehnung an Übung c.

e Individuelle Schülerlösungen in Anlehnung an CV auf Seite 155.

C2 Interviews

(i) **a** *Die Schüler/innen führen Bewerbergespräche in Kleingruppen durch. Bei leistungsstarken Schülern ist es erstrebenswert, von der Vorlage auf Seite 156 abzurücken und ein freies Bewerbungsgespräch zu halten.*

(k) **b** 4, 8, 12.

c Individuelle Schülerlösungen

C3 The Green Card – a controversial issue

Politische Streitgespräche finden in der heutigen Mediengesellschaft verstärkt im Fernsehen statt. Die Schüler/innen dürften daher mit dieser Art von „Fernsehdiskussion" vertraut sein. Eine möglichst realistische Umsetzung des Rollenspiels erfordert von den Beteiligten einige Vorarbeiten, die im Allgemeinen angesichts der vorgesehenen „Aufzeichnung" motivationsfördernd wirken:

Das Klassenzimmer wird in ein Fernsehstudio verwandelt. Eine Podiumsdiskussion erfordert neben den räumlichen Umbauten auch den Einsatz von einzelnen Schülerinnen und Schülern in technischen Funktionen (Kamera, Beleuchtung, Tontechnik ...); die restliche Klasse beteiligt sich aktiv als Zuschauer an der Podiumsdiskussion, d.h. die „Zuschauer" sollen im Anschluss an die Diskussion die Beiträge für z.B. einen Zeitungsbericht zusammenfassen.

D Grammar revision: Future tense

a 1. I am going to Brussels next week.
2. Our train leaves at 8 o'clock tomorrow morning.
3. How long will you be staying in Philadelphia?
4. Our office opens at 9 o'clock.
5. Wait a minute! I'll help you.
6. I suppose Jane's application is going to be accepted.

b 1. I'll do
2. I'm going to wear
3. I'll have
4. leaves
5. are meeting
6. starts
7. are watching
8. will be enjoying
9. will be over
10. departs
11. I'll be
12. it's going to be
13. it's going to rain
14. I'll need

c 1. My new job as a computer specialist will surely be very interesting.
2. I'm going to apply for a position abroad as soon as possible.
3. My employer is offering me a job in New York next year.
4. I'm convinced that I'll make the right decision.
5. Wait a moment: I'll help you!
6. I expect that the demand for computer specialists will increase.
7. My plane departs at 4:30 p.m.
8. Are you going to apply for the job?
9. I'm going to apply for a job in England.
10. "I'm going to write my application tomorrow." "You'll need some information."
11. Around this time tomorrow I'll be flying to London.
12. "It's snowing! Our plane will be delayed."

File 1 – Civil engineering

a **roof:** clay products, timber, plastics, metals
  frame: concrete, brick, timber, block, steel, sheet materials
  wall: brick, block, concrete, sheet materials, timber
  floor: concrete, sheet materials, timber
  foundation: concrete, brick, block, sheet materials, steel

b
1. partition walls
2. drainage
3. masonry
4. reinforced concrete structures
5. building structure
6. live loads
7. strip foundation / load-bearing walls
8. trench
9. concrete / steel reinforcing bars
10. piers and buttresses / shuttering methods
11. beam
12. span
13. pre-stressed concrete
14. pitched roof

File 2 – Woodworking

A Professions
- ❶ carpenter
  ❷ joiner
  ❸ glazier

B Materials
a ❶ pine
  ❷ maple
  ❸ walnut
  ❹ cherry

b –

C Tools
a ❶ work bench
  ❷ chisel
  ❸ mallet
  ❹ file
  ❺ planer
  ❻ brace
  ❼ clamp
  ❽ keyhole saw

b ❶ saws
  ❷ planer
  ❸ chisel
  ❹ clamps

c
A jigsaw is used for cutting curved and irregular lines or ornamental patterns. An eccentric grinder is used for smoothing a board, sanding edges and polishing surfaces.

D Work processes: Joining wood

a ❶ nails   ❶ sight
   ❷ lath   ❷ shrinks
   ❸ tackers   ❸ loose
   ❹ bonds

b ❶ Kreuzschlitz   crosshead (AE: Phillips)
   ❷ Linsenkopf   raised head
   ❸ Sternkopf   star drive
   ❹ Kopf   head
   ❺ Schaft   shank
   ❻ Gewinde   thread

c –

File 3 – Laser technology

a 1. **false**; laser is an acronym for "light amplification by stimulated emission of radiation".

   2. **false**; lasers can be found in CD players, laser printers, dental drills, high-speed metal cutting machines and measuring systems.

   3. **true**

   4. **false**; they exist at specific energy levels.

   5. **true**

   6. **true**

   7. **true**

   8. **false**; the characteristic laser colour is red.

   9. **true**

   10. **false**; modern lasers can produce pulses with the power of some billion watts.

   11. **true**

   12. **false**; CO_2 lasers are very powerful and are used in industry, for example to cut through steel.

b –

File 4 – Logistics and transport technology

A Logistics

a Logistik ist der Teil des Ablaufprozesses der Versorgungskette, der sich mit der Planung, Durchführung und Kontrolle eines leistungsfähigen, wirkungsvollen Flusses und der Lagerung von Gütern, Dienstleistungen und entsprechenden Informationen vom Entstehungsort bis zum Verbrauchsort befasst, um den Anforderungen der Verbraucher gerecht zu werden.

b –

c 1. arrange for   3. flawless
   2. efficient   4. theft

d 1. transport (noun)   4. coordinated (adjective)
   2. origin (noun)   5. finance (verb)
   3. consumption (noun) 6. insure (verb)

B Modes of transport

a The graph shows very clearly that the roadways are the most favoured mode of transportation in Germany: Whereas the proportions of goods transported by rail, inland waterways and sea freight are basically the same, roadways have to carry more than ten times that much. It is also quite obvious that the trend is to put even more tons on the road, and less on the other means of transport, if you compare the development of the figure from 1997 to 1999. This predominance of road transport in logistics can no longer be tolerated.

b The roadways are the most important mode of transport in Germany.

c *Example:* Most of our roads and motorways are jammed – they simply cannot be called an appropriate mode of transport any more. If I were minister of transport I would certainly try to change this situation. My solution would be to convince more and more companies to transport their goods by train. Taxes on roads and fuel would certainly be very helpful.

d Hier könnten z. B. europäische Länder vorgeschlagen werden, oder aber Länder in Afrika oder Südamerika mit ganz unterschiedlicher Infrastruktur.

e *Pro:* If a change is made in a part there will not be a large stockpile of the parts no longer needed.
Without the need for storage, parts need to be handled only once.
Contra: Any unforeseen difficulty, such as traffic strikes or natural disasters like flooding, can halt production for up to several days, with costs in the millions, until the needed parts are delivered.

f –

Unit 1
Crossword puzzle

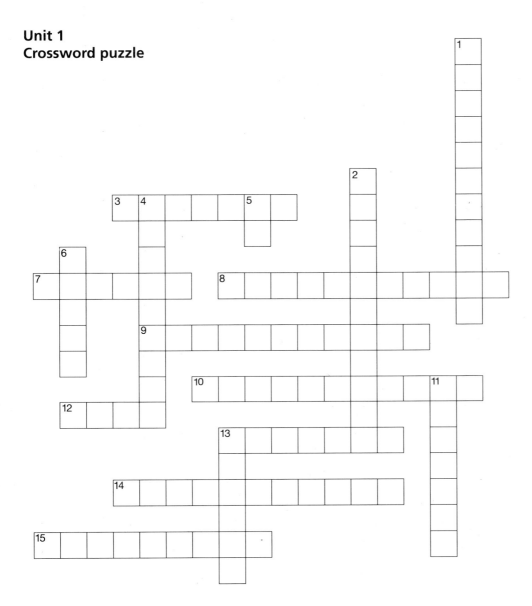

Across

3. a job open at a company
7. give or hand in
8. employment
9. suitable
10. sth. is a ____ if it makes life easier
12. a box or a folder to keep letters or documents in
13. most recent, up-to-date
14. chance
15. a conversation between an applicant and a personnel manager

Down

1. designing and constructing engines and machinery
2. a formal written request for a job
4. obtainable, in stock
5. a short report about your life and career (abbreviated)
6. because of (two words: 3/2)
11. to ask for s.o.'s advice
13. working life

Unit 2
Crossword puzzle

Across

1. to bring something or somebody back to life again
4. if you would like a job offer you have to send an _____
5. you can get information there if you are looking for a telephone number (9/9)
6. a document that tells you what you have to pay
7. a machine that can make copies of documents
9. sure thing
10. hours you work if you work more than you have to
11. to buy
13. to do or say something again
14. office device that staples papers together
15. fees
17. seldom
18. room where people work at desks

Down

1. opposite of an increase
2. noun of the verb "to approve"
3. somebody who produces something
7. American English for British English "full stop"
8. double the radius
12. document signed by two or more parties that states what the partners have to do
16. another way of expressing that the telephone line is busy

Unit 4
Crossword puzzle

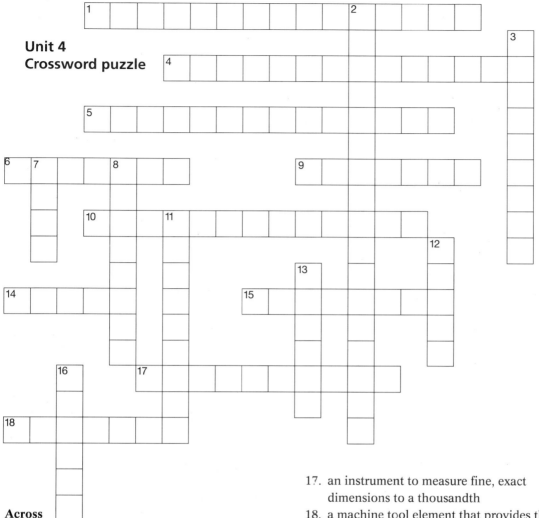

Across

1. a machine tool used to get fine smooth surfaces (2 words: 8/7)
4. a machine tool to work different shapes of flat material (2 words: 7/7)
5. a measuring instrument for inside/outside dimensions, length, diameter and the depth of a workpiece (2 words: 7/7)
6. a part/element of a milling machine that houses the spindle
9. a hand tool to fix or loosen nuts and bolts
10. a power tool used at home or in industry for making holes (2 words: 7/5)
14. a machine tool element that holds cutting tools
15. a lathe component that carries the tool quick exchange
17. an instrument to measure fine, exact dimensions to a thousandth
18. a machine tool element that provides the rotation of a part

Down

2. a handtool which grips, clamps or cuts small pieces of metal (2 words: 11/6)
3. a lathe component that houses the main spindle
7. a device to clamp material for working
8. a hand tool for socket head bolts (2 words: 5/3)
11. the way of rotation that goes to the right
12. a machine tool for working round material
13. you plug an electric cable in here
16. a device that you hold in your hand to protect your face during a welding job

© Ernst Klett Verlag GmbH, Stuttgart 2002. Alle Rechte vorbehalten.
Vervielfältigung zum Unterrichtsgebrauch gestattet.

Unit 7
Crossword

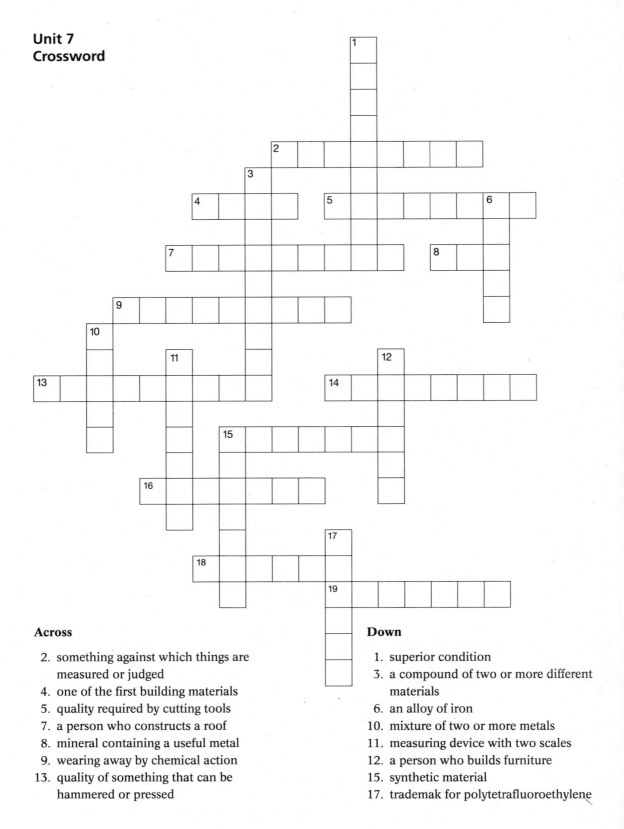

Across

2. something against which things are measured or judged
4. one of the first building materials
5. quality required by cutting tools
7. a person who constructs a roof
8. mineral containing a useful metal
9. wearing away by chemical action
13. quality of something that can be hammered or pressed

Down

1. superior condition
3. a compound of two or more different materials
6. an alloy of iron
10. mixture of two or more metals
11. measuring device with two scales
12. a person who builds furniture
15. synthetic material
17. trademak for polytetrafluoroethylene

Unit 9
Crossword puzzle

Across

2. meat from a chicken or a duck
4. the first meal of the day
8. a list of prepared food that can be ordered in a restaurant
9. meat from a pig
10. where you check in at a hotel
12. the authority that controls and collects fees for the import and export of products
14. where you sleep when you are travelling
15. large city on the east coast of the USA
16. the coming and going of motor vehicles on streets and roads
19. someone who parks your car at a hotel
20. a small car

Down

1. when most people do not have to go to work
3. a travel document
5. guarantee of a booking
6. items that can be drunk with a meal
7. someone who goes on a journey for business or pleasure
11. where planes take off and land
13. filled with something
17. agreement to use something for a certain amount of time for a certain amount of money
18. picture of a letter, sent electronically

Klassenarbeit Unit 3

Text CAD – CAM – CIM

There are various paint programs. With the simple ones the users can draw colourful pictures and print them out or integrate them into a text. If the users are skilled enough, they can create illustrations for their presentations. The more refined programs, such as those for Computer-Aided Design (CAD), are for technical drawing. Complicated components, such as machine parts, can be designed on the screen and shown at any given scale. The created images are 3D models. This is highly advantageous as an engineer or architect can look at a design from almost any angle. This way new machine parts can be designed on screen, and the finished drawing can be printed out with the exact measurements and explanations. Another advantage of electronically designed plans is that they can be sent as e-mail attachments via the internet from one place to another, from the design office of a company in Germany to its manufacturing unit in England or vice versa.

Apart from CAD, there are many more uses for computers in industry. Computers run robots or control automated assembly lines, they are excellent planners and organisers of complicated production processes, and they keep track of materials in stock. This wide field of computer applications is called CAM – Computer-Aided Manufacturing.

The CIM system, Computer-Integrated Manufacturing, integrates all components and functions of a company. From the first contacts with customers to offers, order entry, design, production, shipment, billing, customer service and even after-sales service. CIM is a rather modern concept. It is very efficient, because it controls every aspect of a business and thus increases a company's performance.

264 w

A Vocabulary

a Find a synonym for the following words: VP
1. various (line 1)   0.5
2. skilled (line 2)   0.5
3. create (line 3)   0.5
4. pictures (line 1/2)   0.5
5. exact (line 8)   0.5
6. company (line 11)   0.5

b Find an antonym for the following words: VP
1. simple (line 1)   0.5
2. advantage (line 9)   0.5
3. sent (line 9)   0.5
4. first (line 17)   0.5
5. modern (line 19)   0.5
6. increases (line 20)   0.5

c Explain in your own words:
1. internet (line 10)   2.0
2. robot (line 13)   2.0

10.0 VP

B Questions on the text   VP
                                       S/I
1. What are the advantages of CAD?   2.0/2.0
2. What are the advantages of 3D models?   2.0/2.0
3. What are the advantages of electronically designed plans? 2.0/2.0
4. Give some uses for computers in industry.   2.0/2.0
5. Why is CIM very efficient?   2.0/2.0

10/10
20 VP

Total: 30 VP

Klassenarbeit Unit 4
Tools

There are lots of tools for everybody. Skilled workers use them in their company workshops, apprentices use them in the general workshops where they are trained in mechanical engineering, and DIY-workers use power tools and hand tools at home. If they want to make or assemble a bookshelf, for example, they
5 need a handsaw or a jigsaw, an electric drill, a drill, a screwdriver or some drill bits and some plugs and screws.
An apprentice, who is trained in mechanical engineering, learns a lot about metals and their properties. They either work metal materials manually or with machine tools. For cutting metal bars and plates, they might use a hacksaw. In their
10 basic machine training, they learn how to operate a centre lathe or a milling machine. They are also trained in drilling holes with a column drill, a machine which is indispensable in a general workshop. Another training module is joining. They learn that the joining method used always depends on the property of the materials to be joined. If, for example, you want to assemble thin pieces of
15 sheet metal, you apply the riveting technique, but if solid steel plates must are to be joined, you should weld them.
After their training the apprentices will be skilled workers who have the necessary experience to operate CNC-machines or even computer controlled assembly lines.

225 words

A Vocabulary   VP

I. **a** Give the *synonym* for: company (line 1)   1.0
           apprentices (line 2)   1.0
           to operate (line 10)   1.0
           properties (line 8)   1.0
           to join (line 14)   1.0

    b Give the *antonym* for: to assemble (line 14)   1.0

    c Explain: skilled worker (line 1)   2.0
                        to weld (line 16)   2.0
                                                            _____
                                                            10 VP

II. **d** Which tools do you need?   **1 VP** each

1. For shortening the bars of a metal shelf we need _____

2. For joining thin pieces of metal we need _____

3. For finishing the surface of a wooden table we need _____

4. For drilling holes into a concrete wall we need _____

5. For assembling and setting up bookshelves we need (2x)
   _____

6. For joining metal bars of a garden fence we need _____

7. For deburring the edges of a metal plate we need _____

8. For drilling holes into a metal plate we need (2x) _____

10 VP

B Questions on the text

Answer the following questions **in your own words** as often as possible and **write in complete sentences**:

VP I/S

1. Who uses tools and where do they use them? — 3/3
2. Would you use a hacksaw and a column drill to make and put up a wooden bookshelf? (Give reasons for your answer) — 2/2
3. When would you use a hacksaw and a column drill? — 2/2
4. Is an apprentice able to operate a CNC-machine? (Give reasons for your answer) — 2/2
5. What is important to know in joining? — 1/1

10/10

20 VP

C Grammar

Put the following sentences into **the correct order**:   **2 VP** each

1. the apprentices / have / of training / will / 3 years

2. the milling machine / cleaned / will be / next lesson / by the trainees

3. a new chief executive / the company / get / will / next month

4. tomorrow / will / we / have to / the column drill / repair

5. the visitors / in the morning / arrive / will / at the company / at 9.00

10 VP

Total: 50 VP

Unit 4 Lathe

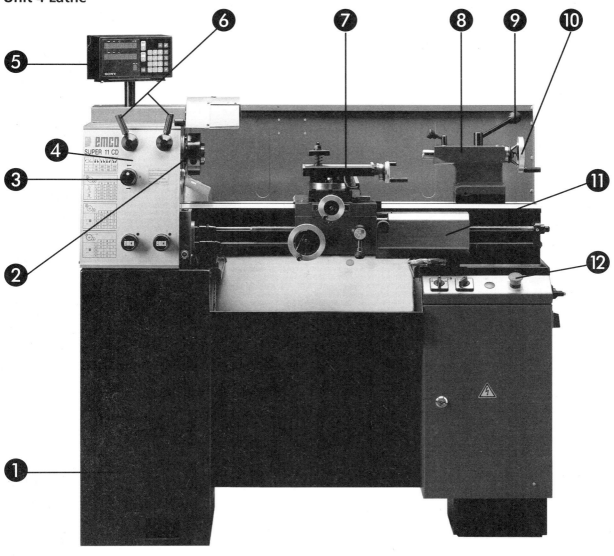

1. _____
2. _____
3. _____
4. _____
5. _____
6. _____
7. _____
8. _____
9. _____
10. _____
11. _____
12. _____

© Ernst Klett Verlag GmbH, Stuttgart 2002. Alle Rechte vorbehalten.
Vervielfältigung zum Unterrichtsgebrauch gestattet.

Unit 4 Milling machine

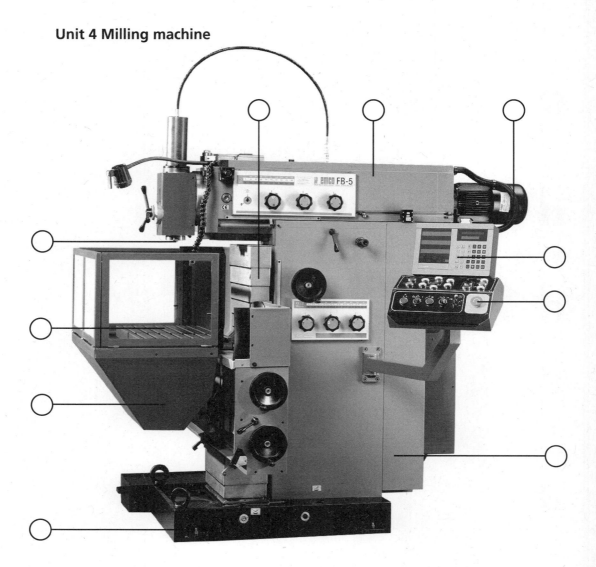

1. base
2. column
3. spindle
4. machine table
5. motor
6. knee
7. overarm
8. emergency off
9. control panel
10. vertical slide

Unit 2 – Zusatzaufgabe

Complete the dialogue by putting in the correct forms of the words in brackets. (Past Tense or Present Perfect?)

After two weeks in Leeds Oliver meets Mary, an English friend he hasn't seen for quite a while.

Oliver: "Hello Mary. I ❶ _____ (not / to see) you for ages. How are you?"
Mary: "Fine, thank you. How are you?"
Oliver: "Well, not too bad. I ❷ _____ (to start) work for Power Engines two weeks ago. I really like my job, it's very interesting. After I ❸ _____ (to finish) my exams a year ago I ❹ _____ (to work) for a car manufacturer in Stuttgart. But I soon ❺ _____ (to decide) to apply for a job at Power Engines. I ❻ _____ (to have) my job interview two months ago and ❼ _____ (to be) lucky to be accepted as an engineer in their research department."

Mary: ❽ "_____ you _____ (to meet) Mr Bill Walker, the managing director? He is really a nice person."

Oliver: "Oh yes, I ❾ _____ (to meet) him the day after arriving in Leeds. He ❿ _____ (to introduce) me to my new colleagues. John Smiley, the research and development director, then ⓫ _____ (to take) me around the company, which ⓬ _____ (to be) very interesting. Since then I ⓭ _____ (to take up) my work in the research department."

Mary: "I ⓮ _____ (not / to be) as lucky as you. After I ⓯ _____ (to pass) my exams last year I couldn't get a job. I ⓰ _____ (to apply) for many jobs in the meantime – but without any success. Things just keep going from bad to worse. So far I ⓱ _____ (to write) sixty applications and last week I ⓲ _____ (to receive) my sixtieth negative answer."

Oliver: "I'm so sorry to hear that. But I honestly think the job situation is improving at the moment, and I really hope you'll get a chance soon."

Unit 9 – Zusatzaufgabe
Nationalities

Put in the correct noun or adjective. Use the box if necessary. Note: not all of the adjectives or nouns in the list can be used in the text. Some of them, however, may come up more than once.

America	American
Austria	Austrian
China	Chinese
Denmark	Danish
Europe	European
France	French
Great Britain	British
Italy	Italian
Japan	Japanese
Korea	Korean
Poland	Polish
Sweden	Swedish
Thailand	Thai
Turkey	Turkish
Vietnam	Vietnamese

It has often been said that the ❶ _____ diet consists mainly of fast food. Anybody who cares to look closer will discover that this is just a prejudice. The reason for it is probably that the thousands of tourists who travel from ❷ _____ countries like Germany, Italy or France to the United States go to fast food restaurants in order to save money.
American cooking is just as varied as ❸ _____ cuisine. Thanks to the immigrants from China, you'll find ❹ _____ food in almost every town. People who like really hot meals may go to ❺ _____ or ❻ _____ restaurants, where cooks from Vietnam or Korea will do a good job for their customers. It is well known that in a ❼ _____ restaurant you will find sushi, which is raw fish with rice and seaweed. Dishes in a Thai restaurant are made of many vegetables and spices which are specifically from ❽ _____.
Everyone in Europe and America feels quite at home with ❾ _____ dishes like spaghetti and pizza. Places serving ❿ _____ dishes like sauerkraut and sausages, however, are rare in the United States. You could say that ⓫ _____ cooking is much more varied than what you and I are used to, and as for fast food, you will find that here in ⓬ _____ too.

Keys
Klassenarbeit Unit 3

A Vocabulary

a 1. varied; different
   2. qualified
   3. design
   4. illustrations; images; drawings
   5. precise
   6. firm

b 1. difficult
   2. disadvantage
   3. received
   4. last
   5. old
   6. decreases

c 1. The Internet is an electronic communication system.
   2. A robot is a computer controlled machine tool.

B Questions on the text

1. You can draw complicated objects like machine parts on the monitor at any given scale/dimensions.

2. The designers/architects/engineers can look at the designed object from all sides/various angles, and the complete drawing can be printed with all measurements and explanations.

3. They can be sent by e-mail attachments around the world and back, and they can be received the same way.

4. Computers are used for robots and assembly line control, in CAD, CAM and CIM.

5. Because it provides a total control of every sort of business, and helps to improve a company's efficiency this way.

Keys
Klassenarbeit Unit 4

A Vocabulary

a 1. firms
2. trainee
3. to handle/to work at
4. character
5. to bond/to assemble/to fit

b to disassemble/to take apart

c 1. That's a worker who has had a training in his/her job and who has got a lot of experience.
2. To weld means to unite two pieces of metal under an extremely high temperature.

d 1. a hacksaw
2. riveting tongs and some rivets
3. a sander.
4. a hammer drill
5. an electric drill and a screwdriver
6. a welding torch.
7. a file or an angle grinder.
8. (a vice,) an electric drill and a twist drill.

B Questions on the text

1. The tools are used by either skilled workers in the workshops, by trainees in the general workshops, or by DIY-workers at home.
2. No, I wouldn't. I'd rather use a handsaw and an electric drill and some screws.
3. These tools should be used for cutting metal plates or bars and for drilling them in a workshop.
4. Not at the beginning. Only after his training when he is a skilled worker.
5. In joining it's important to know the properties of the materials.

C Grammar

1. The apprentices will have three years of training.

2. Next lesson the milling machine will be cleaned by the trainees.

3. Next month the company will get a new chief executive.

4. We will have to repair the column drill tomorrow.

5. The visitors will arrive at the company at 9.00 in the morning.

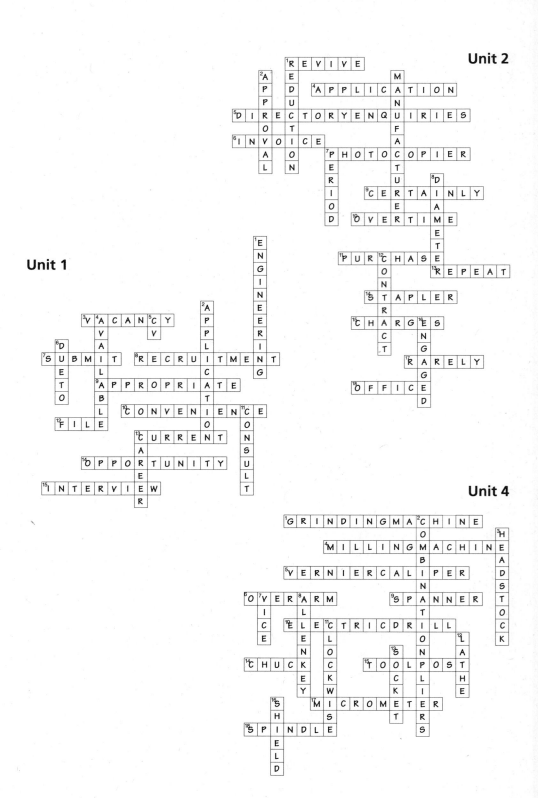

Unit 7

Unit 9

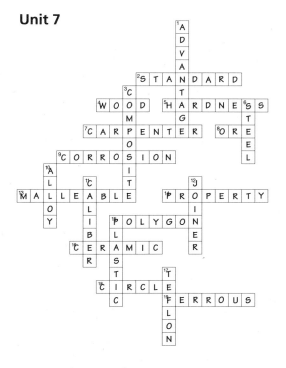

Key: Unit 4 - Lathe

1. frame
2. main spindle
3. motor reversing switch
4. headstock
5. control panel
6. speed selection lever
7. toolpost
8. tailstock
9. tailstock locking lever
10. tailstock handwheel
11. saddle and cross-slide
12 emergency off

Key: Unit 9 - Zusatzaufgabe Nationalities

1 American
2 European
3 French
4 Chinese
5 Vietnamese
6 Korean
7 Japanese
8 Thailand
9 Italian
10 German
11 American
12 Europe

Key: Unit 2 Zusatzaufgabe

1. haven't seen
2. started
3. finished
4. worked
5. decided
6. had
7. was
8. have/met
9. met
10. introduced
11. took
12. was
13. have taken up
14. haven't been
15. passed
16. have applied
17. have written
18. received

Some differences in vocabulary between British and American English:

British	American
aeroplane	airplane
aluminium	aluminum
boot (of a car)	trunk
bonnet (of a car)	hood
mobile (phone)	cell(ular) phone
cross-head (screw or screwdriver)	Phillips
flex (a flexible insulated electrical cable)	cord
lavatory	washroom, toilet
lift	elevator
lorry	truck
petrol	gasoline
rear mirror (of a car)	rear-view mirror
savoury	salty or spicy, not sweet
subway	underpass, underground pedestrian passage
underground	subway
windscreen	windshield

Some of the spelling differences can be grouped and are consistent, others are isolated.
Where the British have **-ou** – the Americans make do with just an **-o**:

col**ou**r	col**o**r	hon**ou**r	hon**o**r
harb**ou**r	harb**o**r	fav**ou**r	fav**o**r
flav**ou**r	flav**o**r	sav**ou**r	sav**o**r

Where the British have an **-re**, the Americans write **-er**:

cent**re**	cent**er**
fib**re**, fib**re**glass	fib**er**, fib**er**glass
met**re**	met**er** *(note exception: The British do spell it "meter" when they are referring to a device that measures, e.g. parking meter, gas meter, postage meter.)*
mit**re**	mit**er** *(= "Gehrung")*

Where the British use a **c** for the noun and an **s** for the verb (licen**c**e, licen**s**e; practi**c**e, practi**s**e), the Americans are content with an **s** for the first, with a **c** for the second.
The British tend to double the end consonant consistently (usually the **-l**) when adding **-ing** or **-ed**, e.g. refuel**l**ing, travel**l**ing, cancel**l**ed, but the Americans do this only when the syllable directly preceding the **-ing** is stressed: e.g. compel**l**ing, control**l**ing; unfortunately. There is even a case where the reverse is true: British = benefi**t**ing, American = benefi**tt**ing. The British also spell the word for Schmuck jewel**l**ery, the Americans jewelry, and the word for (Auto-)Reifen is spelt **t**yre in British, but **t**ire in American English.
The British do tend still to spell certain words with an **s** where the Americans use a **z**, e.g. analy**s**e, capitali**s**e, characteri**s**e, organi**s**e. However, as early as 1979, a British English Dictionary stated that the **s** was an "acceptable variant spelling". Thus, the best one can do is to decide on one form and be consistent.
Finally, the British use the American spelling of progra**m** when it refers to the computer, but retain the spelling progra**mme** when speaking about the television or the agenda of a meeting.